HEAT RESISTANT

How to fireproof your leadership.

BY PETER ASHLEY

Cover design and book design by Abby Shepard.

ISBN 978-1098394301

HEAT RESISTANT

How to fireproof your leadership.

BY PETER ASHLEY

Contents

FOREWORD

I first met Peter Ashley in November of 1994 when I was only a few years into my tenure as the Fire Chief in Chapel Hill, NC. Peter was pursuing his master's degree at the University of North Carolina and wanted to conduct a research project for his thesis. This was not at all unusual as Chapel Hill being a college town, we had under-graduates and graduate students coming to the Fire Department on a regular basis for interviews, studies, photo-journalism assignments and other school-related projects. Little did I know at that time, I would spend 25 years as Chapel Hill's Fire Chief (at the time I retired - the longest serving municipal Chief in the North Carolina) and that Peter and I would have interactions for the next 25+ years on the subject of leadership.

You see, I never intended to stay in Chapel Hill for that long. My original intent was to stay three to 5 five years and then pursue a Fire Chief position in a much larger Department. At one point I actually accepted a Fire Chief position in another Department (1995) and resigned from Chapel Hill but 24 hours later withdrew my resignation. That's a whole other story for another time! When I became Fire Chief in 1990, I was coming from a larger municipal department in Florida where I had been second in command for five years (Deputy Chief) and figured I had the role and responsibilities of being a Fire Chief figured out. I had been acting Fire Chief there several times and was close to the Chief, enabling me to observe all of his actions and decisions. So, I arrived at the Chapel Hill Fire Department (CHFD) thinking I had all the tools necessary to lead. Boy, was I wrong!

After evaluating the status of the CHFD for the first several months, I told the City Manager it would take two years to turn the Department around in terms of services, methodology, technology and training. Five years later I was still working on that original plan. I now understand (and one of the reasons I teach leadership to Fire Officers) that the Fire Service does a poor job of preparing rising officers for the challenges of executive-level leadership. The common approach is somewhat akin to teaching people to swim by shoving them in the deep end of the pool. Some learn to swim, and some drown. I guess I learned to swim but it wasn't easy.

I attribute any success I had at leading to several factors. The first having a strong sense of personal values and a solid work ethic taught me by my parents. That has always served me well. The second factor was having the benefit of good mentors throughout my career. Starting as a rookie firefighter when an older driver-engineer took me under his wing and taught me how to get along and gain respect in the Fire Service. As my career evolved there were other fire officers and instructors who took an interest in my career and guided my development as a young fire officer and later as a chief officer. Mentoring is in my opinion the third leg of learning along with education and experience – and is crucial to success at any level in any discipline and especially important for leaders. The last factor

I believed contributed to my success was always trying to surround myself with people and staff members who were smarter and more driven than me. When you play a sport with someone better than you, you improve and that is true in leadership.

I have had my share of mistakes, bungles, regrets and screwups in my leadership roles and some were very public and painful. If anyone wants to learn from my leadership success, they must also learn from my leadership missteps and fumbles. I certainly feel like leadership is never mastered, it is only practiced and hopefully improved. Someone once told me learning leadership is like learning to play a violin in public. Every screech, scratch, squeal and wrong note is heard by everyone. But I tried to learn from those scratches and recover to do better the next time. Leadership roles in any field of endeavor is not for the faint-of-heart and you have to want to lead. It cannot be taken lightly or with a nonchalant approach when others are counting on you. This truth is magnified in emergency services leadership where lives, communities and livelihoods depend upon your leadership. I must say that despite some difficult times and regrets, I enjoyed the role of being a leader and I loved the people I worked with. I guess that is why I stuck with it so long. When I retired as a Fire Chief, I told my team that I wanted to be remembered for always trying to do the right thing for them. I owed my firefighters and fire officers a lot because their support enabled our collective success in the CHFD. And to "pay it forward" for all the valuable mentoring I received in my career, I now try to serve as a mentor for those who have ambition to lead.

Thank you, Peter Ashley for your interest in my career, for our enlightening discussions along the way and for helping others through your writing and mentoring to be successful leaders. Peter has great insights into the role and responsibilities of leaders. God knows we need better leaders in every aspect of our society today. Any progress, change, or advancement does not happen without leadership.

LEAD ON!

Chief Dan Jones, Ret.

INTRODUCTION

This book is not about me or my leadership style. If it were, it would be a lot shorter and likely less compelling. I'm skeptical of books written by successful leaders that feature themselves as the subject. Rather, this book is focused on the lessons we can all learn from a great leader who would never say that he was a great leader. Notice I did not say famous. Fame does not make a leader great. In fact, it can have the opposite effect. No, the leader featured in this case study – spanning more than 25 years – is truly great because of his approach to leadership, his choices and his character. There is a reason that leadership is one of the most researched and examined topics in business and academia – it's central to how we live, what leaders we support, what values we hold, and what futures we envision. In much of the literature, leadership has been studied primarily from a business or political perspective.

So what does it mean to fireproof your leadership? It means building trust and engagement with your teams. It means fostering creative problem-solving in a safe environment. It means giving employees a genuine sense of ownership in decisions that affect them. By following the principles and actions laid out in this book, leaders will become more heat resistant and will be able to handle tough times more effectively.

Twenty-five years ago, I conducted an in-depth study of how transformational leadership manifested itself in a non-business situation. The study focused on how transformational leadership was expressed within the context of a fire department. Of course, living in a PC (Post-COVID) world, the lessons captured in this book are even more relevant, as leaders must be even more resilient.

The goal of the original study was to examine how a transformational leader made sense of (cognitively evaluated) different situations, and how that cognition affected communication to followers. The case study also examined the influence of leadership on the followers in terms of their role identities – basically how the followers viewed themselves enacting their roles as firefighters. The original study was conducted at the Chapel Hill Fire Department using observation and in-depth interviews. The leader's sense-making processes were examined in the context of five critical leadership events. In terms of the leader's influence on followers, interview analysis was conducted and ultimately revealed three categories of role identities in which the firefighters viewed themselves. Finally, follow-up interviews were conducted with Chief Jones to assess how well his leadership choices held up over time.

Results from the first research question revealed that a leader's sense-making is most heavily influenced by prior experience, his or her goals for the organization, and salient situational features. The most highly valued and prominent cluster of role identities of the firefighters was that of "responsible community servant." Firefighters also strongly valued their "growing professional" role-identity cluster. Findings suggested that transformational leadership and role identities can be valuably linked and require further study.

So why now? Why – after 25 years – did I revisit not only this topic, but the actual leader who was the focus of the case study? I was so impressed with the results this leader achieved after his first two years as Fire Chief, that I wanted to see if those leadership principles help up under scrutiny and over time. Chief Jones recently retired after 25 years of leadership of that same fire department. Succeeding as a Fire Chief for so many years communicated to me that he was the real deal. And unconstrained by the need for academic jargon and rationale, I was compelled to reconnect with the Chief Jones and conduct follow-up interviews to not only validate my initial findings, but also to learn more about the long-term effects of transformational leadership.

Since Chief Jones' "retirement", he has become a sought-after consultant and trainer across the country. The focus of much of his training has been leadership in the fire service, but also how that type of leadership translates into other applications and settings. His particular style of leadership articulated in the original study has proven to be effective, but also has evolved into a more nuanced, situational approach. Many hard lessons were learned that doubtless refined his leadership strategies and tactics. One thing is clear; the principles that guided Chief Jones 25 years ago, not only have withstood the test of time, they have considerable applicability to today's leaders.

This book will set the context by revisiting the original study into transformational leadership as manifested in Chief Jones, but it also provides clear insights and concrete actions today's leaders can adopt. Leadership is an ever-evolving concept, with new theories and "magic bullets" cropping up on a regular basis. This book will show how tried and true, proven strategies offer the best path to successful, authentic and sustainable leadership. In essence, leaders who wish to "fireproof" their leadership – enable it to withstand the inevitable heat of challenging situations – need to look no further than the example set by Chief Dan Jones.

CHAPTER 1

THE PERENNIAL IMPORTANCE OF LEADERSHIP

The Shaping of a Leader

We are all influenced throughout our lives by parents, siblings, teachers, coaches, mentors and countless others. Influence is just that – influence – not control or orchestration. It's also not inherently positive or negative, but rather the sum total of the experiences and interactions we've had that shape our perspective, choices and behaviors. Chief Jones was fortunate, by his own recounting, to have many positive influencers in his life. From an early age, Chief Jones learned the value of hard work, perseverance, consistency and integrity.

"My first awareness of leadership was in the Boy Scouts, with a scoutmaster who was a former Marine Corps drill instructor," Chief Jones recalled. "He became a scoutmaster because he missed the Marine Corps. That was probably my first-ever exposure to real leadership, and I stayed with the Boy Scouts." It was early in Chief Jones' life that he was drawn to more military settings for leadership – perhaps a precursor to his desire to work in the fire service. Even though he was drawn to military-type settings, Chief Jones' view of leadership was greatly expanded over his lifetime. His basketball coach made a long-lasting impression. "He was strict and set high expectations, but he was also caring and went out of his way to do things for other people. Although I didn't realize it at the time, he was demonstrating servant leadership."

Chief Jones intended to go to law school, but soon realized he disliked it. A friend invited him to hang out at a fire station, and when he got a glimpse of that life, he skipped classes the next day and applied to four of the largest fire stations in the area. Although he did not intend to make a career out of firefighting, he found he had a real aptitude for it, particularly for administrative positions. A long and successful career was proof Chief Jones made the right decision.

When asked what contributed to his success and longevity in a challenging discipline, Chief Jones credits many mentors over the years who taught him how to learn, fail and lead.

As a rookie firefighter, he took me under his wing and in the evenings after dinner, we would sit in folding chairs out front of the fire station and he would talk to me about how to get along with everybody in the fire department better. He was probably my first professional mentor.

There are so many factors that shape leaders and leadership. Mentors, good and bad bosses, peers, family, faith are but a few. For Chief Jones, mentors and experiences taught him so much about leadership. An avid reader, Chief Jones also digested volumes on leadership to deepen his understanding. In the pages ahead, readers will get an in-depth look at Chief Jones' leadership style and choices during his signature assignment at the Chapel Hill Fire Department.

The Questions Driving the Study

I said to myself...when I came here that my job was to get this fire department up and running using its own talent to the point that technologically and methodologically it is state-of-the-art and change oriented and pushing forward. When it begins to go on its own, I can slip out the side door and no one will notice that I left. The process will continue and whoever comes in as fire chief will have a forward-thinking organization. That is my objective to get it to the point that it does it on its own and I am not needed anymore.

– Chief Dan Jones, 1994

Chapel Hill Fire Chief Dan Jones captured the essence of effective, transformational leadership with this simple, yet powerful statement that he gave me when we had our first interview more than 25 years ago. The key notion expressed in this quotation is that effective leadership involves, at least in part, turning followers into their own leaders thus enabling them to drive an organization forward. This movement forward is driven by re-shaping the organizational members' work-related meanings, thereby creating a new organizational identity. This quotation also provides a preliminary look at how Chief Jones makes sense of leadership situations and contexts. Additionally, Jones discusses plans for major organizational change, which is a key feature of transformational leadership. In the original study, the effects of transformational leadership were discussed in terms of the firefighter's idealized roles, or their role identities. In a 2018 interview with former Chief Jones, he captured effective leadership with a simple, yet profound statement. "Leadership is earned, not appointed. And it is earned repeatedly."

Transformational leadership, as articulated here, is leadership that encourages followers to rise above their own expectations and do more than they originally thought possible and do so in a changing environment. This organizational change occurs, in part, by the leader changing the followers' meanings for work and their place in it. Furthermore, organizational change must be fostered and developed by the leader through his or her modeling the desired behaviors. Chief Dan Jones enacted such transformational leadership as he oversaw a period of extensive change – over a quarter of a century – at the Chapel Hill Fire Department.

Leadership research has typically explored leader traits, behaviors, and performance outcomes. Much of the research involving followers has focused merely on follower satisfaction and performance. However, as conceptualizations of leadership have evolved, there has been a shift in emphasis toward other dimensions of leadership. For example, researchers have suggested that characteristics of the leadership context, not merely of the leader, affect the type and subsequent success of the leadership strategy employed. Furthermore, there has been an increase in the analysis of followers' responses to leadership on a deeper level, beyond satisfaction or follower performance.

A critical conceptualization of effective leadership is known as transformational leadership, which has been defined in several ways emphasizing different elements. For example, Burns (1978) originally defined transformational leadership as a positive leadership style used to raise the moral awareness of the recipient. This increased moral awareness often translated into enhanced follower performance. Burns' (1978) process-oriented view of transformational leadership occurs when the higher order needs of the followers are met. Unlike transactional leadership theories of yore, transformational leadership moves beyond behaviors and actions that merely cater to basic needs (Yukl, 1989).

The conceptualization of transformational leadership that guided the original study was more similar to Bass' (1985) view, which emphasizes the leader's effect on subordinate behavior. Bass suggests a leader's positive effect on followers is enhanced when the leader has gained admiration and respect from followers. This clear link to followers is a critical element of transformational leadership. Leadership, as studied here, is considered transformational to the extent that Chief Jones attempted significant organizational change, primarily through transforming followers' meanings for work, the organization, as well as their roles.

Bass and Avolio's (1994) four "I's" of transformational leadership were applied as a basis for assessing the existence of transformational leadership at the Chapel Hill Fire Department. The four "I's" are idealized influence, individual consideration, intellectual stimulation, and inspirational motivation. The components mentioned earlier are more general qualities of transformational leadership and are represented in the detailed descriptions of the Four "I's," which appear in the next section. In order to study the implementation of transformational leadership, it was necessary to select an organization in which that type of leadership was being enacted.

Many years ago, I heard Chapel Hill Fire Chief Dan Jones speak about his experiences as the new Fire Chief in Chapel Hill. His comments stayed with me as I continued to learn more about leadership, and the importance of leadership communication in different contexts. Chief Jones spoke of many of the changes he intended to enact at the station, and he spoke of his vision for the Chapel Hill Fire Department. Two basic elements of transformational leadership, change and vision were apparent in Chief Jones' description of his experiences while fire chief. Once I decided that leadership communication was to be the focus of the original study, I was compelled to approach Chief Jones, hoping he would allow me to conduct a study about his leadership style and behaviors. Using transformational leadership as the guiding leadership conceptualization seemed reasonable because of the preliminary evidence suggesting his use of it. Furthermore, I was interested in discovering whether other transformational qualities were evident in Chief Jones' leadership.

Another factor in the design of the original study was the heightened interest in the study of the sense-making processes of leaders (e.g., Smith & Peterson, 1990; Meyer, 1990). Previous conceptualizations of leadership as skills, traits, or styles provided an inadequate explanation of leadership choices. Other theorists suggested that leadership situations and traits are more predictive when the leader's interpretation of them is analyzed (Smith & Peterson, 1990). Consequently, the process that leaders use to construct leadership situations and make decisions became a vehicle for researchers to gain more insight into leadership. This shift toward understanding leader sense-making processes in context, along with my conceptualization of transformational leadership as centering on negotiated the work-related meanings of followers, helped define my methodology. In order to explore fully the sense-making processes of Chief Jones, an interpretive approach seemed most appropriate.

Rather than simply address subordinate satisfaction or subordinate assessment of leader success, as ample prior research has done, the original study focused on followers' identities-particularly their perceptions of themselves in various roles encountered at work These self-perceptions were used to demonstrate the effectiveness of Chief Jones' leadership. Specifically, I applied McCall and Simmons' (1978) Role Identity Model to explore the influences of Chief Jones' leadership choices on their identities.

The integration of transformational leadership theory and the Role Identity Model offered some intriguing insights. Most importantly, it fit well within the conceptualization of transformational leadership as the process of attempting organizational change through transforming followers' work-related meanings. My re-conceptualization of transformational leadership suggested that an important dimension of it is influencing followers' identities. Thus, the concept of role identities was an appropriate tool in assessing Chief Jones' influence on the firefighters because role identities represent the meanings followers' have for themselves performing idealized roles. It is these roles that transformational leadership attempts to influence.

Employing an interpretive methodology provided important advantages to conducting the original study. Theorists often described organizations as cultures in which meanings are negotiated, viewing leadership as the management of organizational meaning (Pfeffer, 1981; Smircich & Morgan, 1982). This cultural approach to organizational research encouraged researchers to employ interpretive methods in explaining leadership in those cultures (Trujillo, 1982; Van Maanen, 1991). The increase of interpretive, qualitative research on leadership indicated that leadership was increasingly being viewed as contextual. Interpretive methods, which included primarily interviews and observation, provide a deeper understanding of the leadership setting.

The overarching purpose of the original study was to extend understanding of transformational leadership by exploring the sense-making and communication of someone attempting to enact it. More specifically, I hoped to accomplish this goal by using interpretive methods to study leadership in context. An additional goal was to integrate previously unrelated theories-transformational leadership and McCall and Simmons (1978) Role Identity Model-as a means of developing an under-emphasized dimension of transformational leadership; the influence on followers' identities. These goals led to the formulation of two hypotheses.

Question One

What are the sense-making processes and communicative choices of a leader enacting transformational leadership?

This first research question addressed Chief Jones' leadership in terms of how he made sense of specific leadership situations and how his sense-making influenced his choices. To explore his sense-making, Smith and Peterson's (1990) model was applied. This model will be explained more fully in the next section.

Question Two

In what ways are followers' role identities influenced by the enactment of transformational leadership?

The second research question focused on how Chief Jones influenced his followers' identities. The reaction of the subordinates to the leader's communication in terms of its influence on the development and subsequent prioritization of their respective role identities was the focus of this question. This research question incorporated the perspectives of the subordinates on a deeper, more personal level than previous studies of satisfaction and performance. Further, this question addressed a more complete definition of transformational leadership by examining how meanings for work and roles at work are negotiated and created.

Summary of Key Research

In this section, some of the literature on the major phenomena examined in the original case study will be reviewed. Many of the references are taken from the early days of studying transformational leadership. This research was the basis of the original case study and is vital to understanding whether the theories the research articulates has stood the test of time. More contemporary research is also included as another method of validating this case study. First, leadership theory and research, including a more detailed discussion of the various conceptualizations of transformational leadership, will be discussed in order to clarify the conceptualization guiding this study. In addition, the first area of research reviewed will include how the sense-making processes of leaders have become increasingly important to leadership research. Second, the Smith and Peterson (1990) event processing model will be explained and offered as the guiding model for analyzing Chief Jones' sense-making and communication. Third, McCall and Simmons' (1978) Role Identity Model will be elaborated on as the theory that guided the analysis of the firefighters' interviews. Finally, this section reviews literature about the interpretive paradigm, drawing on both organizational culture and symbolic interactionist research in order to clarify its appropriateness as the paradigmatic template of this thesis.

Leadership has been one of the most frequently researched topics among organizational and management scholars. Throughout the course of the study of leadership, researchers have redefined and revised their explanations of leadership. Bass (1990) reviews thousands of studies and theories of leadership as defined in many different ways. Despite the extensive coverage that leadership has received, new perspectives continue to dot the landscape as scholars and practitioners try to understand leadership better. This section considers the basic developments in leadership theory from some of the earliest perspectives to very current ones in an attempt to contextualize the use of transformational leadership in this study.

Although there have been myriad studies of leadership, many questions remain for practitioners and scholars alike. Those who research and write about leadership must first demonstrate an inadequacy in current research that their new research addresses. Thus, leadership studies often can be somewhat predictable and repetitive. Rost (1991) describes this predictability as a ritual undertaken by the researcher in which he or she first suggests that current research is inadequate and second, proceeds to summarize past research. According to Rost, it is the manner in which the summary of previous leadership research is presented, that leads the reader to the false conclusion that substantial progress has been made in understanding leadership. Bennis (1959) indicated that leadership is less understood and more studied than almost any other topic in the behavioral sciences. It is this lack of finality, of certainty, that drives researchers to continue developing theories and studies in an attempt to "know all there is to know" about leadership.

Early research was dominated by so-called "great-man" theories that suggested people were born with physical and psychological characteristics that enable them to be effective leaders. These qualities, if possessed, made one a likely candidate for a leadership position. Despite the hundreds of studies conducted in the 1930's and 1940's designed to pinpoint the "magic bullet" of leadership, no consistent traits emerged that would guarantee leadership effectiveness (Yukl, 1989). There were of course traits that emerged as somewhat predictive, but none that would predict success for everyone. Predictions made by trait theories were unreliable because any correlation between traits and leadership effectiveness was weak and often inconsistent (Hackman & Johnson, 1991; Yukl, 1994). As a result, frustrations emerged with this and similar views of leadership. Early trait approaches emphasized personal characteristics; however, more recent trait research examined how traits can lead to specific actions or behaviors (Yukl, 1989). Despite the realization that traits are a factor, however, trait theories alone were inadequate to explain leadership.

Merely possessing certain traits could not adequately explain leadership effectiveness given the many contexts in which leadership occurs. This realization led scholars and practitioners to shift their attention to situational factors, or contingencies that affect a leader's success. Fiedler's (1967) LPC Contingency Model took the trait perspective to another level and began to examine situational factors that affected the relationship between traits and effectiveness. Other situational theorists posited that there were various factors in a given leadership situation that inhibited or encouraged effective leadership. Characteristics of the subordinates, task, and environment are among the variables that scholars predicted could interact to influence leadership effectiveness. House's (1971) Path-Goal Theory, Hersey and Blanchard's (1976) Situational Leadership Theory, Kerr and Jermier's (1978) Leadership Substitutes Theory, and Yukl's (1989) Multiple Linkage Model are a few of the theories that addressed situational factors influencing leadership effectiveness. Although situational models offer more complex conceptualizations of leadership than did trait theories, research guided by them still resulted in somewhat ambiguous findings (Yukl, 1994). Furthermore, their complexity actually works to inhibit their effectiveness in real managerial settings (Yukl, 1994). In other words, most managerial work occurs in a fast-paced environment; consequently, complex situational models often are not useful guides to leadership study and practice.

At the time of the original study, a relatively recent and very promising perspective on leadership emerged: transformational leadership. Having become quite a buzzword in academia and corporate America alike, the term "Transformational Leadership" requires a bit of historical explanation. Downton (1973) originally used the term "transformational leadership," when he contrasted it with transactional leadership. Barge (1994) indicates that transformational leadership theory was developed largely in the 1980s coinciding with an increasingly popular view of organizations as cultures (McKinney, 1991; Pacanowsky & O'Donnell-Trujillo, 1983; Pfeffer, 1981; Putnam, 1983; Smircich, 1983; Smircich & Morgan, 1982; Smith & Peterson, 1990; Trice & Beyer, 1984; Trujillo, 1992; Van Maanen, 1991). As scholars began to study organizations as cultures using interpretive methods, the focus on symbols and meaning prompted some to re-evaluate the role of leadership in these "cultures." To understand the development of transformational leadership research, it is necessary to (a) define it more thoroughly and (b) re-conceptualize it from an interpretive perspective.

Transformational leadership has been defined as leadership that goes beyond merely exchanging rewards for work and attempts to change followers' attitudes about both themselves and the organization (Bass, 1990a). Bass (1990b) states that such leadership,

> *Occurs when leaders broaden and elevate the interests of their employees, when they generate awareness and acceptance of the purposes and mission of the group, and when they stir their employees to look beyond their own self-interest for the good of the group (p. 21).*

Bass further contrasted transformational leadership with transactional leadership, which was premised on exchanging rewards for work-related effort. Hersey and Blanchard's (1977) Situational Leadership Model and House's (1971) Path-Goal Model are well-known theories that are based on transactional leadership assumptions. In moving beyond the simple exchange of rewards for work, transformational leadership strategies seek to induce more significant changes in followers' attitudes about the organization by addressing their higher-level needs (Bass, 1985). Burns (1978) also contrasts transformational leadership with transactional leadership in terms of the values involved in each process. He argues that transactional leadership values only aspects of the exchange process, and not the values associated with the inspiration of followers (Yukl, 1989). Furthermore, "Bass (1985) defines transformational leadership primarily in terms of the leader's effect on followers" (Yukl, 1989, p. 211).

Transformational leadership has been studied considerably since its infusion into both communication and management research (Bass, 1985; Bass, 1990a; Bass, 1990b; Bass & Avolio, 1993; Bass & Avolio, 1994; Bennis & Nanus, 1985; Burns, 1978; Holladay & Coombs, 1994; Rosenbach & Mueller, 1988; Tichy & Devanna, 1986; Zorn, 1991). Although many researchers have actually used the term "transformational leadership" in their studies, others have used different parlance to describe similar leadership forms (e.g., Kouzes & Posner, 1987; Kotter, 1990; Rost, 1991). These other studies provide further evidence of the impact of transformational leadership concepts to leadership research. The concept was further refined in terms of modeling the way, inspiring a shared vision and challenging the process (Kouzes & Posner, 2002).

In many ways transformational leadership has morphed into what we now call employee engagement. By engaging employees through effective leadership communication, a transformational environment is more likely to be created. "The moment we totally commit ourselves and begin giving 100 percent, a certain momentum develops. People naturally gravitate to those who are committed and start working in the same direction" (Colan, 2009). That's the essence of heat resistant, transformational leadership.

In a pivotal study, Bass and Avolio (1994) suggested that transformational leadership consists of more than a simple exchange of rewards; rather, it consists of leader behaviors and follower responses that are summarized in what they term the four "I's". These four "I's" reflect both desirable leadership behaviors and the consequent follower responses expected in the enactment of transformational leadership. The four "I's" are idealized influence, inspirational motivation, intellectual stimulation, and individualized consideration.

Idealized influence is a response in which followers admire and respect leaders as a result of leadership behaviors such as sharing risk and being consistent. A leader also induces this response through placing his or her needs below those of the followers. Inspirational motivation occurs when leaders inspire and motivate through providing meaning to the work of the subordinates by setting clear goals, building team spirit, and displaying optimism. The leader intellectually stimulates the followers by encouraging them to think creatively and solve problems in new ways. This response is garnered when the leader solicits followers' ideas and withholds public criticism of followers. The individually considerate leader is a good listener who provides opportunities for growth of the individual organizational member through acceptance of individual differences and personalized interaction (Bass & Avolio, 1994).

These four "I's" still embody transformational leadership because they emphasize organizational change through a transforming of the individual. The leader's enactment of the four "I's" encourages the follower to develop in more substantial ways, both personally and professionally, than does enacting transactional leadership. Thus, we have a definition of transformational leadership that includes the uplifting of followers and the inducement of significant organizational change.

Many of the previous studies focused primarily on behaviors or traits of transformational leaders and on subordinate satisfaction with the leader. Although transformational leadership is still evolving, its application has been limited by its continued focus primarily on traits and behaviors. Another trend in leadership research at the time was a focus on leaders' sense-making processes. Rather than focusing primarily on leadership traits and behaviors, theorists from this perspective investigated how leaders interpret and make choices in their leadership situations. For example, Smith and Peterson (1990) provide an overview of recent research into leadership sense-making processes and offer a model for understanding these processes. They argued that leadership is a series of interpretive processes during which leaders choose responses after considering several factors, such as prior experience and situational features. The specific model of sense-making that guided the original study is the Smith and Peterson (1988) Event Processing Model.

Smith and Peterson's Sense-Making Model

Smith and Peterson (1988) offered a model for understanding leadership in terms of leaders' sense-making and choice processes. They countered the popular notion at the time that leadership was "something which a leader does to a follower," and suggest that their "intention is focused upon the leader as actor, not upon the subordinate as follower" (Smith & Peterson, 1988, p. 14). The model they presented focused on "the processes whereby a leader decides whether or not to act in a given situation and if so, what type of action is likely to be enacted" (Smith & Peterson, 1990, p. 46).

Their model based on leadership sense-making and action involves three components: a) the experienced situation, b) choice processes, and c) behavioral choice. According to Smith and Peterson (1990), a leader must first experience a leadership situation. An experienced situation begins with the perceived event. This event can range from a specific instance or can refer to an entire leadership-subordinate relationship. Perceived events typically precipitate choice processes and behavioral outcomes. Factors influencing this perceived event include goal-directed and attention-interrupted processes. Smith and Peterson (1990) indicated that leaders initially make sense of leadership situations in terms of their goals or in response to being interrupted.

The other factors that affect how a situation can be experienced are schemas, attributions and salient values. According to Smith and Peterson; "schemas can affect goal-directed processes by structuring the information sought and used in goal-directed activity" (p. 51). Factors involved in the attribution process include "rewards and punishments, the closeness of supervision, expectations about future performance, and aspirations held for a member" (Smith & Peterson, 1990, p.52). Salient values involve the desirability of various event outcomes according to the personal characteristics of the leader and situational factors. These salient values "may affect leadership behavior choice by affecting the attractiveness of different outcomes" (Smith & Peterson, 1990, 52).

Based on the situation as experienced, a leader engages in two kinds of choice processes before taking action: a programmed choice or motivated choice. Programmed choice processes are those that take place in a low level of consciousness, rather than involving a deliberate thought-process. Alternatively, motivated choice processes are rational processes through which a leader considers and determines a desired course of action. Smith and Peterson (1990) note that either process is an extreme response, and less likely to occur in pure form. They indicate that "other semi-programmed, semi-rational processes could be shown between these extremes" (Smith & Peterson, 1990, p. 53).

Within the motivated choice process, Smith and Peterson (1990) note three other processes at work. These processes:

> *Include a leader's effort-to-performance expectancy (E), namely, the judgment that the various leadership and non-leadership behavioral alternatives being considered could be successfully enacted; the performance-to-outcome instrumentalities (I), namely, judgments that the various leadership behaviors would lead to desired outcomes; and judgments as to the immediate and long-term values attached to those outcomes (V) (p. 53).*

Leadership behaviors encouraged by these expectancy-based processes occur infrequently, and most likely only when the "leadership choice is unprecedented or has obvious, very significant consequences for the person making the choice" (Smith & Peterson, 1990, p. 53). So, in most cases, programmed choices are more prominent.

Their model of event processing offered a useful tool to analyze the sense-making processes of leaders. Furthermore, it offered particularly beneficial insight into the study of transformational leadership, because of the emphasis on leader choice (i.e., implementation of the four "I's") in transformational leadership theory. Using the Smith & Peterson (1990) model, it was possible to understand a leader's sense-making by first selecting various events that occur, and second, assessing factors involved in the leader's decision to act. The specific aspects of the model emphasized in analyzing leadership events will be discussed at the beginning of Chapter Three to frame the discussion of the first research question. With a better understanding of the model guiding the research question about leadership sense-making, attention turns to the theory and model which guided the analysis of the second research question.

McCall and Simmons' Role Identity Model

Identity has been an important concept in communication research for many years. As with leadership, researchers have developed theories and views of identity in both interpersonal and organizational contexts. Goffman (1959) provided an early and pivotal description of identity in terms of self-presentations. These presentations were viewed as performances in which we all engage as we communicate with others. Goffman's dramaturgical perspective viewed life as a performance or a drama in which we perform various roles. It is through these self-presentations, Goffman believed, that people attempt to manage their impressions and communicate with others. Borrowing from Goffman, McCall and Simmons (1978) developed their role identity theory. McCall and Simmons argued that humans imagine and enact idealized views of themselves in various social roles. Less performative in nature than Goffman's self-presentations, these role identities are developed and nurtured by the extent to which certain role identities are supported.

The notion of identity found a significant place in organizational research as well. Cheney and Thompkins (1987) described this connection in terms of organizational identification, or the extent to which organizational members feel like a part of the organization. Tajfel and Turner (1985) argue that people place themselves in numerous social categories, among which, is organizational membership. Although the concepts of identity and identification made headway in organizational research, Ashforth and Mael (1989) suggest that they were still under-represented in social science research at the time. This research continued here with the application of the McCall and Simmons (1978) Role Identity Model to an emergency service organization.

The basic construct of McCall and Simmons' (1978) model is the role identity, or the "character and the role that an individual devises for himself (sic) as an occupant of a particular social position" (p. 65). McCall & Simmons (1978) also posited that role identities provide meaning in our lives as we attempt to live up to the demands of those idealized roles. "In fact, they give the very meaning to our daily routine, for they largely determine our interpretations of the situations, events, and other people we encounter" (McCall & Simmons, 1978, p. 67). According to McCall and Simmons (1978), changes in one's role identities can have a significant impact on his or her behavior. Consequently, examining the influences of transformational leadership on role identities makes sense, and is consistent with one of primary goals of transformational leadership, which is changing followers' work-related roles. Particularly relevant is the idea that transformational leadership changes the way followers view themselves in the organization.

McCall & Simmons (1978) further indicate that role identities are arranged in a hierarchy of prominence, or levels of importance and accessibility. There are several determinants of the prominence of a certain role identity. These are a) the level of commitment one gives to his or her various role identities, b) the extrinsic rewards one receives from enacting various role identities, c) the intrinsic rewards received from enacting various role identities, and d) the support from relevant others, such as superiors. According to McCall & Simmons (1978); "paramount among these determinants of prominence, however, is the degree to which the individual has committed himself (sic) to the particular contents of this role identity" (p. 75). The influence on role identity prominence that is particularly relevant to this study of transformational leadership is "the degree to which one's view of self has been supported by relevant alters – one's boss, peers, relatives..." (McCall & Simmons, 1978, p.75). Thus, the nature and frequency of support offered by others can, and often will, affect the amount of commitment one gives to a role identity.

In addition to prominence, McCall and Simmons (1978) indicated that the situational salience of role identity performance is affected by perceived opportunity of the successful enactment of a role identity. Since my original study went beyond simple 'yes' or 'no' questions geared toward assessing satisfaction, and into the realm of self-perception, it was necessary to use a philosophical approach consistent with the type of information I was seeking. The following section discusses literature on the interpretive perspective to demonstrate its appropriateness as a guiding paradigm for the study.

Interpretive Perspective and the Cultural Approach

A key premise underlying the thesis of this study was that a transformational leader's influence on his or her followers can be usefully assessed in terms of the development of or change in the followers' role identities. This influence and the assumptions behind it are consistent with a symbolic interactionist view of communication. Symbolic interactionism suggests, in part, that people create meanings in their world through interaction (Blumer, 1969). The three fundamental assumptions of symbolic interactionism are a) human beings act toward things based on the meanings those things have, b) those meanings are created through social interaction, and c) those meanings are handled through perceptual processes. The leadership situations Chief Jones operated in created opportunities for the negotiation of shared meaning between leader and follower. Furthermore, the development of role identities can be viewed through a symbolic interactionist lens as how followers create meanings for "self" – in this case, at work. Thus, the conceptual framework guiding this study is consistent with a symbolic interactionist perspective.

The interpretive paradigm, which is philosophically consistent with symbolic interactionism focuses on the interpretations of the individual organizational members (Blumer, 1969). In contrast to the functionalist approach, the interpretive paradigm views human beings as voluntary creators of their social reality (Burrell & Morgan, 1979). Furthermore, this framework views organizations as highly subjective creations of its members. Thus, "organizational reality is socially constructed through the words, symbols, and actions that members use" (Putnam, 1982, p. 200). My original study's clear emphasis on the re-construction of an organization through changing followers made the interpretive framework a logical choice.

To study an organization using this framework, it was necessary to delve into the lives and the related interpretations of organizational members. The resulting "thick description" (Geertz, 1973) enables the researcher to understand more fully the perspectives of the members which in turn gives the researcher a superior understanding of the interpretations and shared meanings of the individual organizational members. Considerable interpretive research on organizations has been done (Pacanowsky & O'Donnell-Trujillo, 1983; Pfeffer, 1981; Putnam, 1983; Smircich, 1983; Smircich & Morgan, 1982; Smith & Peterson, 1988; Trice & Beyer, 1984; Trujillo, 1992; Van Maanen, 1991), validating its promise as an organizational perspective. While most studies dealt primarily with either the leaders or the subordinates, my original study integrated the sense-making processes and communicative choices of leaders, and the interpretations of and reactions to those choices by followers.

Transformational leadership is also consistent with a symbolic interactionist perspective on communication. Transformational leadership largely involves the re-shaping of followers' meanings for the organization and themselves through leader the actions embodied in the four "I's." Furthermore, the meanings created in the organizational vision must be negotiated and agreed upon. It is through this change in shared meaning that transformational leadership, role identities, and symbolic interactionism become inter-connected. Much of the previous transformational leadership research is mechanistic or functionalist, rather than interpretive (e.g., Rosenbach & Mueller, 1988). Studying transformational leadership and role identities to examine the meanings negotiated and shared in the Chapel Hill Fire Department was consistent with symbolic interactionism, and an approach that lent itself to the use of interpretive methods.

Both transformational leadership and symbolic interactionism are also consistent with viewing organizations from a cultural perspective. Researchers have demonstrated that leadership and the cultural approach can be usefully combined (O'Donnell-Trujillo, 1983; Pacanowsky & Putnam, 1983; Pfeffer, 1981; Smircich, 1983; Smircich & Morgan, 1982; Smith & Peterson, 1988; Yukl, 1989). The cultural approach stresses the creation of shared meanings of organizational members. To understand these meanings and how they are created, researchers must attempt to access organizational members' sense-making process. Since the cultural metaphor stresses that "organizations are viewed as systems of shared meanings and beliefs" (Pfeffer, 1981, p. 1), it served as a useful perspective for studying the sense-making processes of organizational members, including leaders (Smith & Peterson, 1988). To understand the perspectives of organizational members better and, most importantly, to understand those perspectives in context, qualitative methods were required. Methods common to interpretive research include interviews, observations, and use of historical context (Anderson, 1987).

Summary

The purpose of this chapter was to provide the research underpinning the original case study. It's important to note that considerably more research has been conducted on transformational leadership, and the previous section reflects the highlights of that research as it pertains to this book. By articulating the research questions and reviewing key literature, the context for this case study should be clearer.

Chapter Two describes the target organization, the Chapel Hill Fire Department, and the methodological procedure that was followed in collecting and analyzing data. Chapter Three analyzes and discusses my findings regarding the first research question. Chapter Four considers the results of the second research question. Chapter Five focuses on the how the leadership choices made 25 years ago have been validated and supported, and the effect this process has had on the Fire Chief featured here. I conclude with a look at the limitations of the original case study, directions for future research, and my final comments.

CHAPTER 2

EXAMINING LEADERSHIP UP CLOSE

This chapter presents a description of the context and the methodology used in conducting the original study and is divided into two major sections. The first section has two purposes. First, it describes some of the unique leadership challenges posed by fire service organizations. Second, it elaborates on the status of the Chapel Hill Fire Department at the time this study was conducted, including information about the size and structure of the station. The second major section describes the procedures, data collection and analysis employed in this thesis and provides a rationale for those choices.

I chose to conduct the study at the Chapel Hill Fire Department for two reasons. First, to address the research questions discussed earlier, I needed to find an organization in which transformational leadership was being attempted; this seemed to be the case at the C.H.F.D. Second, I was interested in conducting the study in an organization unlike those that have been the setting for most previous leadership studies (such as corporations or government agencies). As an emergency service organization, the C.H.F.D. promised to add unique dimensions to the study of the implementation of transformational leadership.

Study Context and Participant Profiles

This section discusses some of the unique challenges posed by emergency service organizations, particularly fire departments, in terms of both leadership and scholarship. This section also describes the Chapel Hill Fire Department in detail so that the context for this study can be understood better.

Emergency Service Management

Emergency service organizations, due to their unique characteristics, provide an interesting backdrop for the study of leadership. Despite this, the emergency service setting has been an under-tapped source of data. The vast majority of leadership studies have been conducted in non-emergency organizations. Furthermore, there had been no studies of transformational leadership conducted in emergency organizations at the time of this original study. Although previous non-emergency service studies contributed significantly to our understanding of transformational leadership, it is possible that they had a limited the scope of the theory. It makes implicit sense that leadership in emergency organizations is very different from leadership in other contexts.

In fact, there is research positing that managing an emergency service, such as a fire department, creates unique leadership challenges (Bryan & Picard, 1979; Hickey, 1979; Thompson, 1979; Ulrich, 1979; Jones, 1987; Drabek, 1990; Carter, 1993). For example, Hickey (1979) suggests that the nature of fire service places certain limits on what type of organizational structure a fire station can use. Furthermore, Hickey (1979) discusses many of the management options available for fire services that take into account the logistical problems and time constraints that are prevalent in the fire-fighting profession. Ulrich (1979) discusses different management approaches in the fire service that meet the specific objectives set out by the fire service. Henry and Shurtleff (1987) compiled chapters contributed by Chief Dan Jones and other fire service experts that address specific management challenges faced by fire departments such as time management, role of the company officer, and stress in the fire service. Drabek (1990) uses twelve successful managers of emergency services as a basis for his book of fifteen strategies that emergency managers can use such as constituency support, media relations, and outside experts in order to increase the legitimacy of the emergency organization. Carter (1993) suggests that the paramilitary setting and culture affect the communication patterns within the organization.

The gist of all this research is that emergency service organizations are characterized by factors that can inhibit the implementation of effective leadership. For example, leaders in such organizations typically operate under tremendous time constraints that make leadership communication especially challenging. The rigid, often militaristic structure of emergency service organizations can inhibit encouragement of individual growth that is now considered essential to effective leadership, particularly transformational leadership. These characteristics had several implications for the study of transformational leadership; including the inherent difficulty in implementing transformational leadership in an emergency service setting.

Transformational leadership is leadership that, among other things, "involves an appeal to followers to transcend immediate self-interests for the sake of some greater cause" (Zorn, 1991, p. 80). Successfully making this type of appeal is an important component of effective leadership in many organizations; however, nowhere is that truer than in emergency service organizations. .

The Chapel Hill Fire Department

At the time, the Chapel Hill Fire Department comprised four stations spread throughout the city. Organizationally, the Chapel Hill Fire Department is structured, like other such organizations, in a para-militaristic, hierarchical fashion. Chief Jones was the head of the organization, followed by two Deputy Chiefs and an Administrative Officer. The Administrative Officer, or Staff Chief, has both the secretary and fire mechanic as direct reports. The Deputy Chief of Prevention, or the Fire Marshal, supervises the Fire Inspector. The other Deputy Chief is the Deputy Chief of Suppression, or the Operations Chief. The rest of the chain of command extends from the Deputy Chief of Suppression. Below that position, there were three Assistant Chiefs who each command their own shifts. Each shift comprised the use of four Captains, one for each station, as well as firefighters and fire equipment operators (FEO's). At each of the four stations, there were usually two firefighters and one FEO on duty at all times. In total, there were 11 captains, 10 FEOs and 25 firefighters. Chief Jones (1994) indicated that the department was somewhat non-traditional in that it employed more minorities and women than many other more traditional departments.

In terms of overall staffing, there were 55 full-time positions and 20 part-time positions. The firefighters worked rotating work shifts at all four stations. There were three shifts, referred to as A, B, and C shifts.

The term shift refers not to the 24-hour workday, but to the crew, A, B, or C, to which the firefighters are assigned. These shifts rotated on a 24-hour basis that ran from 7:00am to 7:00am. Each shift, comprising three or four people, would work one day, have one day off, work one day, have one day off, work one day, and have four days off, for an average of 56 hours per week. Based on responses from the interviews, this 24-hour shift was preferred by many over the old system of 10-hour day shifts and 14-hour night shifts.

For the year of July 1, 1993 through June 30, 1994, the Chapel Hill Fire Department responded to 1,688 calls. Of those, 1,503 were emergency calls. The further breakdown of the total number of calls is as follows: 80 structure fires; 205 rescue calls; 588 false alarms; 65 vehicle fires; and 750 miscellaneous responses such as dumpster fires, gas leaks or brush fires. The total fire loss accrued in Chapel Hill for that year was $754,708. In addition to responding to fire calls, the Chapel Hill Fire Department has many other regular functions. These functions included commercial inspections, home inspections and reviewing of fire plans. In that same year, the Chapel Hill Fire Department operated on a budget of $2,595,121. Of that budget, 89% was used to meet personnel costs, and the remainder went to equipment costs and other supplies.

Chapel Hill Fire Chief Dan Jones came to the Chapel Hill Fire Station in April of 1990 from St. Petersburg, Florida, where he had been an assistant chief. Chief Jones spent seventeen years in St. Petersburg moving up through the ranks. In addition, Chief Jones had written articles on leadership, consulted for other departments, and spoken on many occasions about the trials and vicissitude of fire department management. According to Chief Jones (1994), the Chapel Hill Fire Department was 20 years behind the times technologically and was in desperate need of transformation.

Soon after his arrival to the C.H.F.D., Chief Jones drafted a five-year plan of change for the department. In the introduction to this study, Jones referred to the station as "an organization in transition... [Which] experienced its first major organizational changes in more than ten years" (p. 1). Articulating such a plan of change, or vision, is crucial to the enactment of transformational leadership (Bass, 1985). Furthermore, interviews with the Chief indicated that a change-oriented vision continued to guide his leadership (Jones, 1994).

It is clear that emergency service organizations offer unique challenges for the study of the implementation of transformational leadership. The Chapel Hill Fire Department, under the leadership of Fire Chief Dan Jones, was an organization that provided an appropriate context in which to study transformational leadership. The next section presents the procedures followed in conducting this study.

Research Process and Procedures

The general procedure for the original study involved (a) initial interviews with the Chief Jones and selected members of the organization, (b) participant observation, (c) thematic analysis of interviews, and (d) follow-up interviews with selected interviewees. This section describes the interviewees in more detail and discusses the data collection process employed. In addition, the rationale for selecting the data collection strategies is discussed. Finally, the procedure section explains how the data were analyzed, and the purpose of the second round of interviews.

Initial Interview with Chief Jones

Fire Chief Dan Jones was very open to be involved in the original study. I had preliminary telephone conversations with the Chief in October of 1994, to assess his willingness to participate in this study. The initial interview with Chief Jones was approximately one-hour in length and semi-structured to minimize the imposition of my own biases into the interview. Furthermore, Chief Jones appeared very comfortable in the interview, and did not appear to require much structure to stay focused. The semi-structured interview is a useful interpretive tool in gathering qualitative data because it allows the interviewee more freedom of expression. Anderson (1987) suggests that an effective interviewer should set up the interview context, and then allow the discussion to flow more naturally. Anderson (1987) does not recommend completely structured interviews because they tend to focus on the performance of the researcher, rather than on the responses of the interviewee. Dexter (1970) recommends that building a cooperative rapport with the interviewee can be very helpful in conducting a useful interview. The preliminary telephone conversations helped to build a positive rapport. In the initial interview, it was my intention to provide Chief Jones with a framework for our discussion with some specific questions, and then asked more questions that emerged from his comments.

The first face-to-face interview with the Chief, conducted on November 7, 1994, focused on his interpretations of the leadership context within which he found himself upon arrival at the C.H.F.D. Questions in this initial interview probed the condition of the station upon his arrival, what types of goals he set for himself, his staff, and the station, and how he attempted to enact them. I asked him to assess the extent to which he thinks that he has achieved those goals. In addition, Chief Jones was asked to comment on his interactions with the firefighters. For example, he was asked with what frequency he interacted with the firefighters and in what contexts. These questions focused not only on his leadership intentions, but also addressed how he attempted to shape the firefighters' self-perceptions. This interview gave me significant background information about the station, as well as a good indication of the types of changes that he wanted to make. It also gave me a good sense of the context in which Chief Jones operates and laid the groundwork on which a second set of interview questions could be created – ones more focused on the "how and why" of leadership choices discussed in the first interview.

Primary Interviews with the Firefighters

There were 13 firefighters interviewed for the original study. Three were fire equipment operators two were fire captains, and the remaining eight were firefighters. They were also numbered randomly from 1-13 to protect their anonymity. The term FF#, followed by the appropriate number, will denote which firefighter interview is being quoted. The firefighters ranged in age from 25 to 50 years old, with a mean age of 35. The group comprised one white woman and twelve men – of whom ten were white, one was black and one was Asian.

The participants were assured their participation was voluntary and that they were free to withdraw at any time with no negative repercussions. This procedure was essential to make the respondents as comfortable as possible. Upon completion of the primary interview, the respondents were asked if a follow-up interview would be possible. The interviews with the firefighters lasted between 30 and 45 minutes and were semi-structured.

My first round of interviews with the firefighters consisted of rapport building questions focused on general perceptions of the fire department upon their arrival. There was some concern on my part, as well as Chief Jones', that some firefighters would assume that my questions were only about Chief Jones. This was a potential problem for two main reasons: Chief Jones' concern that the firefighters might feel uncomfortable being interviewed about their chief, and my concern for the increased favorable bias that might emerge in interviews solely about Chief Jones. To avoid focusing solely on Chief Jones, I asked them why they became interested in the fire-fighting profession, and what they like best about it. These questions were designed to put them more at ease, which allowed me to shift toward questions probing their perceptions of Chief Jones' leadership, his effectiveness, and on how that leadership affects them. Rapport with interviewees is very important because it increases the likelihood that they will tell you the truth. Not only were these questions designed to put the firefighters more at ease, they were necessary to discover other motivations and influences on their role identities. I was primarily interested in their assessment of any changes in the department that they perceived since the arrival of Chief Jones. In the case of those firefighters who arrived after Chief Jones, questions were re-worded to address differences between their experiences in Chapel Hill and past experiences elsewhere.

To address the role identity issue, I asked questions regarding their perceptions of the various parts of their job or "roles" at the station. I asked them about what Chief Jones did and said upon his or their arrival, and how they perceived him initially. In addition, I asked them to indicate their initial perceptions of their roles to determine which of them had idealized qualities. To isolate various possible role identities, I asked them to describe the different parts of their job that they felt were especially significant, and in what ways Chief Jones affected those aspects.

There is a narrow distinction between roles and role identities, which was made by allowing the firefighters to speak relatively freely about their jobs. This approach was intended to allow the firefighters to identify the roles for which they held valued or prominent role identities. McCall and Simmons (1978) offer suggestions for accessing role identities that are consistent with my methodological choices. While many of their suggestions reflect a quantitative social science perspective, McCall and Simmons (1978) also recommend semi-structured interviews as an effective means of researching role identities.

Use of Observations

During and after the time of these interviews, I spent time observing the department in its day-to-day operations including riding along with them, which allowed me to better understand their environment. Observations included staff meetings, a captain's assessment workshop, training exercises and several hours in and around the interviews at the station. In addition to this time, I spent a full 24- hour shift at Station #1. This time proved to be the most useful observation time because it gave me a more complete sense of the context than simply observing for a few hours at a time. During the shift, I observed and participated in the emergency response training class that went on for much of the day. Chief Jones provided me with a radio receiver for my home that allowed me to keep track of when the department was responding to calls. On three occasions, I responded to a fire scene just as the department was responding. The overall time spent observing was approximately 50 hours. My procedure for taking field notes was the most difficult part of the observation. Much of the time was spent in ways non-conducive to meticulous field-note writing.

The main purpose of the observations was to give me a better sense of what it means to be a firefighter on a practical, day-to-day basis. After seeing the same firefighters working for a 24-hour period, I better understood what it takes to work in the Chapel Hill Fire Department. The direct contact between Chief Jones and the firefighters was infrequent and was assessed most effectively through the interview process. Furthermore, assessing role identities means determining what the individuals perceive as relevant identities, and not just what I observe. However, observing them helped me to see the manner in which various role identities discussed were enacted on a daily basis.

Second Interview with Chief Jones

To verify and refine my original interpretations, and to ask more specific questions about leadership situations, the Fire Chief was interviewed a second time. The second interview took place on February 16, 1995. As indicated earlier, the first interview was designed to assess what had occurred since Chief Jones' arrival. The second interview was guided by my analysis of the first interview. This interview was designed to uncover the rationale behind various leadership choices and situations. With specific leadership situations in mind from the first interview, I was able to address effectively the first research question which considered the sense-making processes and communication of a leader enacting transformational leadership. The second interview was very useful in clarifying many of the sense-making processes and communication strategies employed by Chief Jones. The transcripts from both interviews with Chief Jones were very useful in addressing my research questions because they enabled me to access his thought processes and his leadership choices.

Analytical Framework

Once the data were collected, I thematically analyzed the interviews to answer my research questions. Chief Jones' interview was analyzed, first to determine whether he was enacting transformational leadership and second, to focus on his sense-making of those leadership choices. By assessing the transformational quality of his leadership, and by examining sense-making and communication of specific leadership situations, I addressed research question one.

More specifically, analyzing Chief Jones' goals, the symbolic means through which he enacted them, his accomplishments, and whether he felt successful, provided a greater understanding of how he makes sense of leadership situations. To consider his sense-making processes, it was first necessary to use specific examples that characterized his leadership as transformational. Drawing on the critical incident method as recommended by Query and Kreps (1993), I isolated five leadership situations in which Chief Jones demonstrated transformational leadership. According to the authors, critical incidents can only be extracted if the interviewee directly observed the actual behaviors occurring in an incident. They recommended using open-ended questions that draw rich information out of the interviewee. In the first interview transcript, I isolated those five events to provide more structure and focus for the second interview. It was then possible to analyze specific choices and reasons by which he attempted to enact his vision in terms of the Smith and Peterson (1990) model.

The four "I's" of transformational leadership (Bass & Avolio, 1994) served as the criteria to assess the extent to which Chief Jones demonstrated transformational leadership behaviors. The four "I's" of "idealized influence" (leader as role model), "inspirational motivation" (leader as motivator), "intellectual stimulation" (leader as encourager of creativity), and "individualized consideration" (leader as mentor), imply specific behaviors that indicate the presence of transformational leadership. Although it is clear that transformational leadership involves more than simple behaviors, these guidelines make it possible to assess basic characteristics of transformational leadership. This distinction is important because I did not want to assume that Chief Jones was transformational; rather, by looking at a conceptualization that suggests actions, I determined whether my specific conceptualization of transformational leadership was present in his behavior.

The analysis of Chief Jones' second interview centered more on sense-making in specific leadership encounters or events. The five events, as defined by Smith and Peterson (1990), were selected as critical incidents that demonstrated what I believed to be the essence of Chief Jones' leadership. It would be impossible to analyze or even mention all the possible events that occur at the C.H.F.D., so it was necessary to select a reasonable number for more in-depth analysis. Once these events were selected and described, evidence of the types of factors entering into his choice-making processes were discussed in order to understand both his sense-making and the model better.

The firefighters' interviews were analyzed first by reviewing the transcripts for general and specific descriptions of Chief Jones' leadership. The transcripts were then analyzed looking for idealized roles in which the firefighters viewed themselves. Examples of these role identities included; community servant, educator, and fire suppressor. Role identity themes were isolated in this study by using Owen's (1984) criteria for thematic analysis.

Owen (1984) suggested that three criteria needed to be met for a "theme" to emerge in discourse. The criteria are: Recurrence, which refers to the same idea emerging in two or more places using different language; repetition, which extends recurrence by referring to the same wording being used; and forcefulness, which is the amount of vocal inflection used in expressing certain statements. These criteria served as a useful framework in which to determine the presence of defensible themes. However, the criterion of forcefulness was not a significant factor in my analysis. As I interviewed the fire station staff, I learned rather quickly that firefighters appeared very low-key. I interpreted this not as a lack of enthusiasm but as a characteristic advantageous in an emergency service organization. Consequently, although certain important roles were mentioned repeatedly by many of the interviewees, few changed their vocal inflection significantly.

Follow-Up Interviews with the Firefighters

To refine and verify my analysis of the firefighters' interviews, five interviewees were contacted and asked to verify my interpretations of their original comments. Rather than interview them in a structured way, I reminded them of their comments, explained how I interpreted them, and asked if that was indeed what they intended. The results that I found were discussed with them to increase the validity of my interpretations. The format of the second round of interviews was far more flexible and less structured. The overall consistency of my results was an important factor in determining how many follow-up interviews were necessary.

Summary & Key Takeaways

This chapter provided a procedure and rationale for how the original study was conducted. I believe that the methodology used in was sufficiently rigorous to address effectively my research questions. I interviewed almost half of the firefighters in the department, and I followed up to check my interpretations. I gained many perspectives on the issues that I was addressing. Finally, the consistency of the results provided encouragement for the credibility of the study.

The next two chapters discuss the results and my interpretations of my time interviewing and observing at the Chapel Hill Fire Department. Chapter Three is divided into two major sections. The first section qualifies Chief Jones' leadership style, and the second section examines his sense-making and communication. Chapter Four discusses the emergence of three major role identity rubrics from the interviews with the firefighters. The existence of these role identities is demonstrated and the influences on them, including Chief Jones', are addressed.

CHAPTER 3

COMMUNICATING TRANSFORMATIONAL LEADERSHIP

The first research question asked, "What are the sense-making processes and communicative choices of a leader attempting to enact transformational leadership?" This chapter will provide evidence that suggests that Chief Jones was enacting many of the characteristics associated with the Bass' (1994) conceptualization of transformational leadership, including the Four "I's" discussed in Chapter One. Once it has been established that Chief Jones engaged this type of leadership, attention will shift to exploring his sense-making and communication. Five critical events were selected as the basis for this discussion. The Smith and Peterson (1990) Event Processing Model will be drawn upon as well to answer this question.

Chief Jones as Transformational Leader

Bass' (1994) Four "I's" of transformational leadership, clarified by Kouzes and Posner's (1987) strategies, indicate specific behaviors that can be expected of someone who is leading in a transformational way. The first of these four is "idealized influence." According to Bass (1994) idealized influence occurs when "leaders are admired, respected, and trusted" (p. 3). Although this definition indicates primarily a follower response, Bass and Avolio (1994) imply that such a response is created in part by a leader's behavior. Admiration and respect are earned, in part, when a leader places his followers' needs above his or hers. Furthermore, "the leader shares risks with followers and is consistent rather than arbitrary" in the treatment of his or her followers (Bass, 1994, p. 3). Other characteristics of idealized influence include doing what is perceived as the "right" thing and resisting the use of power for personal gain. These behaviors on the part the leader often result in the follower response of admiration and respect. This admiration results in a desire in followers to emulate the leader. Thus, the leader has influenced his or her followers by his or her idealized behavior.

Throughout my interviews with Chief Jones, many of the firefighters and various documents, I found strong evidence to suggest that Chief Jones provided many of the key elements of idealized influence. For example, Chief Jones indicated that early into his tenure, during a structure fire, he put on the gear and went into the building to help the firefighters. In this instance, Chief Jones demonstrated that he was willing to share the risk of injury or death with his firefighters.

Another example of idealized influence involves the Chapel Hill firefighters' need for new protective clothing. Upon his arrival, Chief Jones noticed that much of the protective gear was outdated and poorly maintained. When the suggestion was made to replace the gear, one assistant chief suggested that due to financial constraints, gear for the officers should be purchased first. Given the fact that the officers use the gear less frequently than do the actual firefighters, Chief Jones ordered that the firefighters gear be replaced before any others. In terms of idealized influence, this example demonstrates placing followers' needs over those of the leader.

In the first interview with Chief Jones, he indicated that the two most important aspects of leadership are "consistency and honesty." Being consistent is another facet of idealized influence. This honesty and consistency manifested itself, in part, through the open-door policy that Chief Jones encouraged. This openness was also one of the five expectations that Chief Jones stated upon his arrival. He stated that "one [expectation] was to promote an open organization, not a secretive one." Thus, there are multiple examples of his behavior that demonstrated idealized influence.

The second "I" of transformational leadership is "inspirational motivation," or behaviors that provide meaning to the work of the followers. "Team spirit is aroused. Enthusiasm and optimism are displayed. The leader gets followers involved in envisioning attractive future states" (Bass, 1994, p. 3). Through the creation of clear expectations, a leader using inspirational motivation encourages followers to reach those attractive future states. Thus, this second "I" in particular embodies the transformational quality of creating a vision.

Upon Chief Jones' arrival, he helped create a mission statement by which the department would operate. The mission statement and the process by which it was created demonstrate the cultivating of team spirit and the envisioning of future states that are indicative of inspirational motivation. Inspirational motivation embodies the importance of a leader creating such a vision. Chief Jones explained:

> *My job as I see it here is to create a joint vision that everybody can buy into and to draw from everybody here and put all of that together and form a vision that everyone has a piece of. Then you create the opportunities, provide the resources and get out of the way.*

Chief Jones also demonstrated inspirational motivation when he communicated five clear expectations to the firefighters upon his arrival. These five expectations, which will be discussed more fully in the next section, indicated that Chief Jones wanted an honest, open organization. Through a clear articulation of those basic expectations, Chief Jones demonstrated elements of inspirational motivation.

The third "I" of transformational leadership is "intellectual stimulation" or encouraging followers to think creatively and re-conceptualize problems. Bass and Avolio (1994) indicate that intellectual stimulation occurs when,

> *Creativity is encouraged. There is no public criticism of individual members' mistakes. New ideas and creative problem solutions are solicited from followers, who are included in the process of addressing problems and finding solutions. Followers are encouraged to try new approaches, and their ideas are not criticized because they differ from the leaders' ideas.(p.3)*

There were several examples that demonstrate this facet of transformational leadership. One of the five expectations that Chief Jones had of the firefighters was that their actions be based on thought. He stated that,

> *Basically, all of us here are going to screw up from time to time. As long as you can explain what your rationale was at the time, then we will back up folks even if they make mistakes.*

This quotation demonstrates intellectual stimulation in that Chief Jones is stating that he refrained from criticizing his subordinates as long as they had a reasonable rationale for their choices.

Furthermore, several firefighters indicated that they were given assignments in which they could choose the best course of action, that they were encouraged to come up with their own solutions to problems. There are, of course, limitations to the application of this strategy in a paramilitary setting such as the fire department. During a fire, for example, there is no time to question orders or to test your own theories. However, this distinction demonstrates that despite the para-militaristic style of the fire department, creativity was still encouraged where possible.

The fourth "I" of transformational leadership is "individualized consideration" which occurs when leaders "pay special attention to each individual's needs for achievement and growth by acting as coach or mentor" (Bass & Avolio, 1995, p. 3). Fundamental to individualized consideration is the creation of opportunities for the followers to learn in a supportive atmosphere in which the followers can gain more personal fulfillment.

At the Chapel Hill Fire Department, Chief Jones demonstrated qualities of this "I" as well. For example, several firefighters said that Chief Jones encouraged them to take classes outside the department, to attend conferences around the country and join local committees. In addition, Chief Jones created special projects for individuals who were interested in those areas. FF #3 indicated that Chief Jones "tried to make opportunities for people to be exposed to more than just what is going on in the Chapel Hill Fire Department." FF #5 stated that, "Here, they say 'you can do that? Great, we have a project for you.'" FF #5 continues:

> Chief Jones put up a notice, 'anyone interested in an EPA project, see me.' I put my name in. Hell yeah, I would like to work on it,

sounds fun.... He said that you have the ball in your court, you handle it. You have the full authority to do what you have to do to get this project done. He took the ball, handed it to me, and gave me all the responsibilities.

In these examples, Chief Jones demonstrated individualized consideration by creating opportunities for individual growth and learning.

To create appropriate projects for individuals, it is necessary for the individually considerate leader to be an effective listener. The Fire Chief's Roundtables were informal discussion groups that the Chief led with a small number of firefighters. These discussions, which will be elaborated on in the next section, and his open-door policy, demonstrated his willingness to listen to his followers' concerns. This statement is confirmed by many of the firefighters interviewed. For example, FF #4 stated that Chief Jones "is a man who is up for new ideas and is willing to listen no matter if it is good or bad. He is going to listen to all sides."

The previous section demonstrated that Chief Jones enacted behaviors associated with transformational leadership." The following two sections specifically address the research question by discussing how first, Chief Jones made sense of his leadership contexts, and second, how he chose to communicate within those contexts.

Chief Jones' Sense-Making and Communication

To demonstrate convincingly that Chief Jones was a transformational leader, I focused on five events that clearly showed Chief Jones' leadership style. Smith and Peterson (1990) indicated that organizational "events" can be virtually anything from one instance to a series of interactions in which a leader interprets and reacts. An "event" is a flexible concept that Smith and Peterson (1990) used to characterize a variety of leadership situations. Once these events were identified, it was possible to apply their model by examining the sense-making and communication employed within each event. After describing the event, I will draw on certain elements of Smith and Peterson's (1990) model to explore Chief Jones' sense-making and communication. By examining Chief Jones' sense-making process and communication choices, clear strategies emerged that can be applied in almost any leadership situation.

One crucial element of the Smith and Peterson (1990) model involves the use of schemas in the processing of information. Given the lack of specificity in Smith and Peterson's (1990) definition of schemas, I drew on Meyer's (1990) specification of situation and strategy schemas. According to Meyer (1990),

Schemata are cognitive structures that organize information about situations, goals, and the kinds of communication behavior that can be used to achieve goals in particular types of situations. (p. 57)

Meyer (1990) further states that "situational schemata contain information about the communicative goal at hand as well as a configuration of relevant situational features" such as expected resistance, intimacy, or salient values (p. 58). Other characteristics of situational schema include personal benefits to and dominance of the speaker. In other words, situational schemas consist of a person's understanding of a given situation and its effect on his or her reaction to the situation.

The other type of schema Meyer (1990) discusses is the strategy schema. A strategy schema "organizes knowledge about a communication strategy that has proven successful under similar circumstances in the past" (Meyer, 1990, p. 58). Essentially Meyer argues that within certain familiar situations, certain previously effective strategies are employed. Meyer (1990) explained:

> *After finding, from multiple situations that contain the same goal and similar configurations of situational features, that a particular strategy consistently produces a successful outcome, an individual will form an implicit rule that takes the form of an association of a schematic representation of the goal and configuration of situational features and a schematic representation of the strategy (p. 65).*

Meyer's schematic dichotomy provided more clarity in the context of the analysis of Chief Jones' sense-making by narrowing the discussion of the Smith and Peterson (1990) model. These models of sense-making are clearly compatible in that Meyer's (1990) model is similar to Smith and Peterson's (1990), but it offers more specific links to schemas and behavioral choices. Furthermore, use of the Meyer (1990) dichotomy provided a more systematic and structured way to apply concepts originating in the Smith and Peterson (1990) model to the five key incidents of Chief Jones' leadership.

First, the event will be described. Second, Chief Jones' goals, situational characteristics, and pre-existing features of each situation will be discussed to provide understanding of Chief Jones' sense-making within the five leadership contexts. Finally, the resulting strategic schema employed in each situation will be analyzed to assess his communicative choices within those situations.

The application of certain parts of the Smith and Peterson (1990) model resulted in some overlap within each event analysis. To minimize repetition when possible, certain clear and overarching situational features will be discussed first. Each leadership event occurred relatively early in Chief Jones' tenure, thus, one very relevant situational feature in each event was his newness on the job. In other words, his newness to the position of Fire Chief is a key factor in each of the five events. The analysis of situational features for each event will focus primarily on those features that are unique to the specific leadership event. Of course, patterns that emerge between events will be addressed.

Event One: The Five Expectations

Within the first week of his arrival, Chief Jones asked to meet with all of the firefighters to lay down five expectations that he had for the behavior of the fire department staff, including himself. The open and interactive presentation of these expectations to a skeptical group of long-time employees served as an important organizational event at the C.H.F.D. Chief Jones explained that although he tried to retain an open mind about specific expectations, he communicated five general ones. Chief Jones explained:

> *I wasn't really sure what their expectations were. I wasn't sure how much I could expect. The first few meetings were pretty tentative, and I didn't have any specific goals set as it relates to objectives to be accomplished, other than the fact that I wanted to get some basic ground rules established. I had some basic expectations. There were five of them that were laid on them from me.... I keep them written down. Honesty and integrity*

*were first. [Second,] Keep your supervisors and subordinates
informed of what is going on. [Third,] Placing the organization
first. Putting the organization agenda ahead of your personal
agenda. And the fourth one was to promote an open organization,
not a secretive, militaristic one. There are no secrets here. And the
fifth one was that actions be based on thought... basically all of
us here are going to screw up from time to time. As long as you
can explain what your rationale was at the time and what your
thought process was, then we will back folks up even if they make
mistakes.*

Through the recalling of these five expectations, several of Chief
Jones' goals were revealed. At one level, each of the five expectations
can be seen as individual goals Chief Jones had, such as expecting
honesty and his desire to have firefighters base actions on careful
thought. Chief Jones elaborated on his rationale for having actions be
based on thought:

*They were used to fire scenes that involved people running around,
shouting and screaming and that sort of thing. One of the first
messages I gave them was that as professional emergency service
workers, we do not get excited in emergency scenes. We should
be calm individuals who are going about our business very
calculating and calm and in control. That was a change they
had to get used to. I think you make better decisions when you
can slow the situation down to where people had the chance to
think their way through it. It keeps emotions from entering into
the decision-process and makes everyone a little more rational
and reasonable about their thought- process. One of the big
things besides putting fires out that the public looks for in the fire*

department is that they want to be reassured that everything is
going to be okay, so a calm demeanor helps tremendously with the
public.

So, the expectations themselves reflect specific goals. In this case, the
expectation that action should be based on thought—and as a result
that behavior in emergency situations appears rational and calm—
reflected a specific, behavioral goal for the firefighters. At another
level, and more pertinent to this analysis, the decision to gather the
group together to convey his expectations, and to do so in a particular
way, reflects a set of goals that he attempted to accomplish in that
communication event.

The apparent overall goal reflected in the setting of the five
expectations was to create a more effective fire department. On several
occasions, Chief Jones indicated his desire to make the Chapel Hill
Fire Department a first-rate organization. He stated:

I wanted it to be a twenty-first century fire department with all
of the modern technology that was available in emergency service.
I wanted to have an aggressive, competent workforce that was
very team oriented. I wanted the department to be highly thought
of in the community.

Chief Jones indicated the importance he placed on having a
successful organization comprising dedicated, competent people.

Another instrumental goal in laying down expectations appears to
have been to establish a common frame of reference within which
everyone at the station could operate (i.e., Chief Jones stating
his desire "to get some ground rules established"). Chief Jones

communicated his desire to the firefighters to promote an open organization (e.g., "there are no secrets here"). In addition to these goals, an apparent goal was for him to establish credibility and overcome resistance to the presence of a new fire chief.

One important situational feature was Chief Jones' realization of the importance of his not assuming he understood the C.H.F.D. context well enough to outline specific goals. Chief Jones needed to remain somewhat tentative until he had a better understanding of the context. This assumption resulted in a lack of certainty about specific expectations for him and the firefighters. This lack of certainty is an important feature of this situation because it encouraged him to be less specific about the content of the expectations. Another relevant situational feature was the entrenched skepticism of the firefighters. Chief Jones explained: "There was a lot of skepticism. A lot of people had worked under a system for so long that stymied growth and restricted development and kept people from trying to put forth ideas and so forth. A lot of them were skeptical that anything would change."

Here, Chief Jones indicated an important feature of the situation that informed his choice of initial conduct. All of his goals and the situational features were factors that affected Chief Jones' strategic response to the situation. Both Meyer (1990) and Smith and Peterson (1988) suggest that situational and strategy schemas are shaped by past experiences. Chief Jones refers to his own past experience as one important source for the schemas invoked in this event. Chief Jones elaborated:

> I guess those [expectations] evolved in a period of time based on expectations I have for myself, one, and two, my own work experiences and organizational experiences in other

organizations, and what I saw people do and not do. When I came here, I had done... quite a bit of consulting... although I had never been the Fire Chief running the organization, I have been an instructor, teaching management, and had spent a number of years telling other fire chiefs how they ought to run their organization. I had a lot of opportunity to think about if I had to do it myself, how would I actually do it. I guess those expectations evolved in that.

Drawing on Smith and Peterson (1990) and Meyer (1990), this quotation can be interpreted as Chief Jones forming a situational schema based on his goals as a new fire chief and other factors of the situation. Although he had not yet experienced that precise leadership situation, Chief Jones had a well-developed schematic representation of such a leadership context (i.e. "a new Fire Chief providing initial direction to an older organization") based on prior similar experience.

Chief Jones' goals, combined with salient situational features (i.e., being new, needing to build credibility, the anxiety of many of the firefighters), encouraged a strategy schema of explaining "ground rules" or general expectations instead of one communicating more specific expectations or goals that might turn out to be inappropriate for this situation. Chief Jones' response to the situation, his strategic choice, was to have an open meeting within which he communicated general expectations. His choices to be interactive and to be general rather than specific in his expectations were strategic communicative choices that were designed to achieve the situational goals discussed earlier.

This first "event", in which Chief Jones demonstrated elements of his leadership sense-making, offers several insights into the sense-making models and to transformational leadership. For example, it is clear from this example that the situational features of this event strongly influenced Chief Jones' course of action, his communication, by guiding his strategic response to a new, yet discernible situation. His desire to promote an open organization and to build credibility was communicated to the firefighters through his laying down the expectations. In other words, the act of laying down expectations is one that is inherently authoritative. Thus, his goal of communicating openness and honesty through laying down five expectations to the firefighters helped build his credibility and demonstrate his leadership style.

The parts of the Smith and Peterson (1990) model that were most useful in explaining the leadership sense-making in this incident are the salient goals and relevant situational features present in the event. Application of the model demonstrated that prior experience in similar situations does help determine the chosen course of action. Furthermore, the major goals that a leader sets during an event helps shape the communicative attempt made to achieve those goals. The goals of the communicator and features of the situation caused Chief Jones to make strategic choices about how he handled this initial and very important leadership event.

This event serves as a good example of effective transformational leadership, which involves transforming followers' views of themselves. Through the five expectations, Chief Jones articulated guidelines that would encourage his followers to improve themselves and their performance through a re-framing of their perception of being a firefighter. Many of the expectations were atypical for the fire service; consequently, the firefighters were asked to consider new possibilities of what it means to enact the role of firefighter. Finally, this event begins to connect transformational leadership and role identities by showing how his leadership attempted to affect the firefighters' perception and enactment of their jobs.

Lessons for Today's Leader

Even though this even happened more that 25 years ago, it's just as relevant today. Leaders are expected to lead by example. Setting clear expectations – that leaders follow themselves – helps followers understand how they can succeed. Expectations clarify what needs to happen in an organization, but it also highlights potential skill gaps. Heat resistant leaders are those who can set clear expectations, hold themselves and others accountable, and remain committed even if the going gets rough.

Event Two: The Creation of a Mission Statement

The second "event" is the meeting in which Chief Jones developed a mission statement for the C.H.F.D. This event is particularly relevant in part because it was one of the first acts in which heengaged. Chief Jones explained:

We had an officer's meeting within the first couple of weeks and one of things I did was use a group process and I acted as facilitator. We, in effect, wrote a mission statement for the department, which you can see on the wall of my office and most of the offices and you will see it in every station. Instead of me dictating that to them, we did it through group process by them answering a series of questions: Who are we? What services do we provide? What do we want people to know about us?

Chief Jones indicated that after the mission statement was created, he asked the officers individually, as he shook their hands, if they could commit themselves to that mission statement. When asked why he chose to use a group process, Chief Jones indicated the importance of including followers in decision-making:

> *As head of the organization I can spend all day deciding where I think we ought to go, but if I don't get at least a majority of the people to buy in on that, we are not going to get there. It is that simple. One person doesn't drive the organization. It takes a lot of people. And until you get all those people to buy in on the plan it just isn't going to happen.*

This rationale is very revealing about how Chief Jones made sense of this particular leadership event. In part, this quotation demonstrates that Chief Jones had a specific purpose in mind when implementing the group mission statement process. Specifically, Chief Jones had several goals (e.g., creating a successful organization) that directed his attention to certain situational features (e.g., his newness to the department and his belief that dictating a mission statement was ineffective) that ultimately activated the strategy schema of using a group process. Chief Jones continued:

> *People who think that they can make things happen in an organization, or make a change occur just by the power of their position, are wrong. I have not seen it happen. Every effective leader that I have observed or been around was only effective because the people that were around them supported what they were doing and worked with them on the same. You can call it what you want. Call it a vision, or call it a shared plan or idea,*

whatever you want to call it, but until the other people buy in on it, it is not going to happen.

In this excerpt, Chief Jones clearly indicated his belief that creating a shared vision was important. From his perspective, effective leadership comes only with follower support, which in turn comes from listening to their ideas. Situational features evident in this excerpt include his belief in change-oriented leadership ("people who think...or make a change"), and his observations of other leaders that support his belief about effective leadership. The strategy schema begins to form when he draws on his prior experience ("I have not seen it happen... Every effective leader that I have observed"). Finally Jones chooses his course of action when he refers to a vision. In other words, when placed in a similar leadership situation, Chief Jones chose to act in a way (using a group process) that enabled him to attain his goals of effective leadership through subordinate support and involvement.

Another rationale for using a group process to create a mission statement was to help the organization form an identity. Chief Jones explained:

That was a way of helping the organization start to form an identity. There was no identity in this organization... a lot of mistrust, a lot of finger-pointing. The only way to get everyone started on the same shoe was to basically say that we are wiping the slate clean and we are starting over, and we are starting over by writing a mission statement and everybody is going to help write the mission statement. And we are going to take all the ideas and then we are going to decide what we want to say in this mission statement together, as opposed to one person coming in and saying 'ok' this is the mission.

This excerpt demonstrated that Chief Jones had several distinct reasons for using a group process to create a mission statement. Here he indicates the importance of giving the organization identity through this process. It is clear that Chief Jones thought about his choice to use group process; consequently, this decision can be viewed as intentional with specific goals in mind. These goals are informed in part by Chief Jones' prior exposure to similar situations. Situational features apparent in this excerpt were the lack of trust in and lack of identity for the organization. Once Chief Jones encountered these features, he implemented strategy schemas that he believed would effectively achieve his goals in that situation. Chief Jones finds himself in a leadership situation in which he must build trust, motivate followers, and encourage them to commit to a vision. With that situational schema in mind, Chief Jones drew on strategic schema based on what he believes will help an organization find an identity. His strategy began to take shape when he indicated there must be a clean slate for the station to form an identity ("we are going to start over by writing a mission statement").

When Chief Jones indicated that he had never seen leadership that was effective based on one's own power, he is implicitly stating that his choice to use group process was in fact based on what he perceived to work in the past. Thus, his strategy schema was continuing to develop out of his knowledge about effective leadership techniques. By indicating his desire to give them the opportunity to create their identity, Chief Jones demonstrated a strategy schema consisting of information about how he perceived identity to be formed most effectively.

When choosing to act in a leadership situation or event, Smith and Peterson (1990) indicate that a leader uses a motivated choice, a programmed choice, or some type of hybrid. In this event, given the strategic nature of his schemas employed and the intentionality of his choice, it is clear that Chief Jones made a motivated choice to use group process in the formation of a mission statement. Furthermore, since this event was planned and not spontaneous, it can be concluded that the goal-directed nature of this leadership situation affected the schemas employed. Chief Jones had specific goals in mind when he chose to use group process, and he drew on previous knowledge about what strategy would be the most effective in achieving those goals.

Chief Jones' desire to help the firefighters form a new identity has implications for the second major research question as well. Clearly, Chief Jones attempted to transform the C.H.F.D. through many different approaches, not the least of which was through the creation of an identity of the group and of the individual members. Thus, the concepts of transformational leadership and role identity are further linked within a leadership event in which Chief Jones led the creation of a mission statement.

Lessons for Today's Leader

The value of creating a mission statement has been long understood by effective leaders and organization for years. It is the process Chief Jones led that is significant, and virtually unheard of in emergency-oriented organizations. Not only did the Chief obtain input from the staff, he personally shook hands with each one confirming commitment. Because every firefighter had a voice in the process, their commitment actually meant something. For today's leader, it's imperative to engage your employees in the process and product of the work of creating a mission statement. Although seeking employee input into decision making is intuitive, it is still not done very effectively in many organizations. When input has been factored in to decisions, those affected by the decisions are more likely to support them or at least abide by the results. That's building heat resistance.

Event Three: Fire Chief's Roundtables

Chief Jones indicated that his arrival was ushered in with some skepticism from the department. He was unknown to the department and needed to interact with them in a non-threatening manner. The event of the Fire Chief's Roundtables, which were essentially informal meetings Chief Jones had with various firefighters, evolved as a non-threatening way to interact with the firefighters. Chief Jones elaborated:

> *I met with the firefighters in informal groups a number of times the first year in what I called the Fire Chief's Roundtables where I would go out to the fire stations, sit at the kitchen table and talk about whatever they wanted to talk about. Whether it was the philosophy of running a fire department or they wanted to talk about how the hose was loaded on the truck, or about what I thought about different colors of helmets for different ranks, or whatever they wanted to talk about. Vacation leave scheduling... whatever was a key issue in their mind; that's what we talked about and for as long as they wanted to talk about it.*

These roundtable "events" were representative of the open organization that Chief Jones wanted to foster. Although openness is not viewed here as a separate event, it was an underlying element of the event discussed here. Chief Jones continued:

It made for some late evenings. But it was the way I was able to, in a very informal and non-threatening way, communicate philosophies of emergency service management and do it on their terms. With their questions, their topics, at their stations, at their kitchen table, and not in a formal training room from a podium and that sort of thing. A lot of times it was without the other senior command officers present so that there wasn't a sense of big brother watching. It was more like, 'what do you want to talk about tonight?' We asked questions or made statements.

Here Chief Jones revealed his initial sense-making of the choice to visit the firefighters on their turf. He was able to more effectively communicate his goals as well as hear their perspectives on the issues. Relevant situational features included the informality of the session, and the importance Chief Jones placed on speaking to them on their terms. The strategy schema emerged in this excerpt as the Chief realized the benefits of informality, such as increased openness and the lack of the "big brother" feel. By excluding other senior commanders, Chief Jones intended to open up a sincere dialogue with the firefighters. Chief Jones indicated that the individual firefighters responded better to informal sessions, Chief Jones explained:

Everybody receives and assimilates information differently. Some people want just the facts. Other people want to have some discussion about what the potentials and what some alternatives are, etc. Everyone has to receive their information differently in order to be comfortable with it. By doing it in informal sessions, it let each person slowly start to develop a perception of me, of the

new management style and philosophy of the department and
let them start to maybe have some pride or self-esteem about who
they were and what organization they belonged to.

Chief Jones reveals several sense-making processes at work. One
relevant situational feature in this excerpt is the fact that people
assimilate information differently. Chief Jones' understanding of this
situation led him to create strategies that he believed would be most
effective in the situation. The strategy of using roundtables developed
in part due to Chief Jones' understanding of how individuals interpret
information. Chief Jones found himself in a new leadership context
that required him to achieve several salient goals. First, Chief Jones
wanted to assuage some of the skepticism of the firefighters. Within
that situation, Chief Jones had a strategy schema that indicated that
informal dialogue was an effective way to alleviate anxiety. In terms
of the Smith and Peterson (1990) model, Chief Jones had certain
outcome preferences that guided his decision to meet with the
firefighters informally.

Through the use of informal discussions, Chief Jones wanted to
encourage the firefighters to develop self-pride and pride in the
organization. By meeting with them informally, and by giving
them a chance to voice any concerns they had in a non-threatening
environment, Chief Jones built their confidence and managed
their impressions of him. The strategy of using informal discussion
groups evolved partly because of the relevant situational features
that were particularly important to Chief Jones. For example, a
situational feature is that the firefighters lacked pride from Chief Jones'
perspective. Consequently, acting on his belief that building pride was

important, Chief Jones chose a communicative strategy based on what prior experienced told him was effective.

Overall this leadership event, referred to here as a series of roundtable discussions, demonstrated that Chief Jones had specific goals in mind when he made that leadership choice. Consequently, this choice can be viewed as a motivated choice in which Chief Jones tried to attain several goals through the strategic choice of meeting informally with the firefighters. This event re-enforced the transformational nature of his leadership, while at the same time demonstrated the relationship of his leadership style and the role identities of the firefighters. Namely, that by helping them increase self-esteem and confidence in themselves and their organization, Chief Jones provided an atmosphere in which the desired role identities of the firefighters could flourish.

By deliberately choosing a non-threatening context in which to address the firefighters' concerns, Chief Jones communicated that the well-being of the firefighters was his primary concern. As with the other examples of Chief Jones communication, this event re-enforced Chief Jones' overall communicative approach of listening to and affirming the firefighters by providing non-threatening atmospheres in which to address their concerns.

Lessons for Today's Leader

Sustaining engagement with employees is no easy feat. Once the initial meet and greets are done, it's too easy to fall back into a top-down communication style. Chief Jones knew this to be true. As a result, he created a standing vehicle to engage his followers on their terms and on issues important to them. This approach provides benefits for both leaders and followers. Followers feel heard and connected, and leaders gain new insights into how to more effectively manage their teams. Creating and maintaining smaller, informal communication opportunities is essential for today's leader to build heat resistance. Fostering trust and cooperation, allaying fears and creating opportunities for synergistic problem solving are proven ways to help leaders navigate their organizations through tough times.

Event Four: The Purchase of New Equipment

Event four involves two separate but similar situations. Upon his arrival, Chief Jones realized that much of the protective clothing worn by the firefighters was out of date. In an addition to using the limited funds for the firefighters' clothing first, Chief Jones also allowed them to have a choice of what to wear. Chief Jones explained:

When we decided to buy protective clothing, we formed a task force made up of people at the lower levels of the organization, firefighters and captains, and we let them pick the style. We got in several samples of different styles and types of clothing from the manufacturers and let them wear it at the working level of the department instead of having it on some staff officer or chief officer. Then we had them tell us which style and company and so forth they wanted to have and that's what we ordered for the whole department and we didn't let any command officer influence the decision. The only thing we said was that it has to meet modern safety standards. As long as it meets modern standards of safety, you can tell us which one you like and that's the type we will buy and that's what we did. We let them choose the protective clothing they are wearing, and they chose based on comfort and functionality.

This leadership situation contains several relevant features that affected Chief Jones' decision-making process. For example, this excerpt indicates that the current uniforms were not in-line with current safety standards. This rather obvious fact does have deeper implications, such as the importance Chief Jones placed on the safety of his firefighters.

In further explaining this decision, Chief Jones indicated several goals in allowing them to select their own gear. He indicated that, not only did he believe that they would be happier with uniforms that they chose, but they would get the message that their opinions and their safety mattered. In terms of their safety being important, Chief Jones indicated that buying the firefighters equipment was critical. Chief Jones continued:

One of the very first things we did to try to emphasize the element of safety being a number one priority was we took what little money we had in the first two budget years and every bit of that when into improving the personal protective equipment of the firefighters. They were operating with protective clothing and breathing apparatus that were way out of date and that is where we put our first money. It went into buying state-of-the-art breathing apparatuses, so they were as protected as technology would allow. That convinced a lot of people that things were going to happen for real.

This quotation not only explains the event, but it does so from a different perspective. Here, Chief Jones emphasizes that choosing to buy their equipment accomplished two other goals. First, it demonstrated that safety mattered, and second, it convinced some people that change was real. Chief Jones strategy schema took shape as he attempted to achieve the several goals he had for the situation. He realized that to communicate the importance of safety, money would have to be spent to ensure the highest standards. Further, to communicate his confidence in the firefighters, it was necessary, in Chief Jones' mind, to allow the firefighters considerable control over their choice of protective apparel. Finally, by allowing them to choose the equipment, and by ordering protective clothing for the lower ranks first, Chief Jones was attempting to accomplish yet another goal. Chief Jones explained:

> *We have got to be careful about how we are spending our money and then they observe you spending that kind of money for things that make your own job easier, more comfortable, or to raise your status symbol. But if you say to them, we have got to cut back this year and they see you do the same thing, then that is different. An example in this organization was we needed to replace everybody's protective clothing or fire-fighting gear and we started by replacing those who needed the gear most of all first. Those who actually do the firefighting. And the chief officers who are less likely to have to actually fight fire, there gear was replaced last. Now that is not true in all fire departments. The gear is replaced on rank and seniority, those with the highest rank or most seniority get the new stuff first. It is reverse order, so that conveys a real message of who is important or what is important.*

This excerpt shows clearly the development of the strategy schema employed by Chief Jones. His choice was informed by situational factors such as who are the primary users of the gear, and what is being communicated to firefighters at other stations when senior officers are placed first. Thus, Chief Jones' prior experience informed his choice to purchase the firefighters' gear first. His desire to protect the lower ranks first served as an important factor in shaping his strategy for action. The other similar event involved the purchase of a much more expensive piece of equipment. Chief Jones elaborated:

> *On a grander scale, we bought a ladder truck two years ago. We had an old ladder truck that needed to be replaced. It was way out of standard and it really wasn't safe to use anymore. We put a group together made up mostly of captains and firefighters and let them write up the specifications. The only restrictions we put on them were a couple of things like it had to have the capability of at least 100 feet and it had to be able to pump... some of those basic types of things. We had a budget of $500,000 to work with. We let them write the specs and choose the bid that was awarded so they spec'd the truck based on their experience about what worked best and what functions and that is what we went with. The truck that we bought was not the truck I would have personally picked out because I have a personal preference for a different type of truck, but the personnel who are going to use the truck here are not me. We basically spent $500,000 on the advice of the folks at the most functional levels of the department and not the command structure and management levels.*

Chief Jones' decision to allow his subordinates to spend $500,000 on a truck that met their requirements – not his – demonstrated a certain level of confidence that he had in them. When asked why he chose to let them select the truck, Chief Jones explained:

Because they use the equipment; I don't use the equipment. The Deputy Chief doesn't use the equipment... although we are responsible for the management of the department and protection of the community at large; those broad responsibilities are shared with the lowest levels of the organization. They understand what's necessary in order to provide that protection and they are the ones who actually have to use the equipment. They are the ones that have to ride it twenty-four hours a day. I ride in a Ford sedan and not in a ladder truck. I don't have to operate the ladder truck. They are the ones who would be expected to rescue people off the tops of buildings with it and they are the ones expected to get it into narrow streets of the university... so it ought to be something they are comfortable with. I could write the specs and dictate to them what kind of ladder truck we would have, but they would still have to operate it, so I want to let them spec it and then they are operating something they designed.

In this excerpt, there were certain relevant situational features that affected Chief Jones' leadership choices. For example, because Chief Jones drove a sedan and not a fire truck, it made sense that his opinion is less relevant than those who actually operated the trucks. Chief Jones assessed his own transportation needs when determining who should decide on a new ladder truck. His choice of a strategy began developing as he realized that the firefighters would be happier and perform better with a truck of their choosing.

In terms of a schematic analysis of the event described above, it is apparent that Chief Jones encountered similar situations in that he seemed well aware of his intended goals for the event. Consequently, Chief Jones made a strategic choice to allow them to choose the truck based on his belief that such a choice would encourage higher satisfaction and effectiveness in his subordinates. Throughout the previous four examples, certain salient values of Chief Jones have continually been demonstrated. For example, it was important to Chief Jones that firefighters were given a voice in decisions that affected them. In addition, Chief Jones valued efficiency and effectiveness, and attempted to achieve them through his leadership choices.

Lessons for Today's Leader

The critical event of allowing the firefighters to select their equipment, and even a $500,000 truck was virtually unheard of in emergency management organization. But the message to his followers was unmistakable: I trust you and I value your opinion. Today's leader can look for creative ways to truly empower their employees with decisions that actually matter, ones that affect their daily lives. Not every organization can allow employees to make decisions on such a significant financial scale, but were possible, today's leaders should look for opportunities to allow employees to make decisions that affect them on a day-to-day basis. By building a sense of ownership, employees will feel more valued and engaged.

Event Five: Entering a Burning Structure

The last event featured Chief Jones temporarily relinquishing his management post and joining in a fire fight with the firefighters. As indicated earlier, this situation, as do the other four events, demonstrated transformational qualities of his leadership. This event was particularly interesting for two reasons. First, this example represented Chief Jones leadership strategy in the field, not just at the station. Second, unlike the other events, there is a more spontaneous quality to this situation than in the other more planned leadership choices. His entering the fire scene was one example of how Chief Jones modeled the way for his firefighters. Chief Jones described the scene:

There was a bad house fire and there was a crew on the second floor trying to fight their way into it. I put on breathing apparatus and went up to the second floor with them. I crawled up close to the officer in charge and said something to the effect of "how's it going captain?" He said, 'who in the hell is this?' I said, 'Jones.' For a minute, he had to stop because he didn't know who Jones was and he didn't expect Fire Chief Jones, to be in the building with him.

This situation depicted what Smith and Peterson (1990) refer to as a situation where attention-interrupting processes are used. In previous situations, Chief Jones may have chosen to respond in a similar manner, recalling a particular strategy schema; however, this instance was thrust upon him. Previous events demonstrated how Chief Jones planned strategies based on his assumption of their effectiveness; however, in this situation, Chief Jones made a spontaneous choice.

Despite the fulfillment of Chief Jones' personal goal of continuing to fight fire, this event revealed other sense-making processes at work. Chief Jones indicated that he felt that joining the firefighters in a burning structure was very motivating to them. It also increased his credibility. He explains that, "if they realize you are willing to do what they have to do, they are more willing to listen to your philosophies and ideas of how things should be done." This quotation demonstrates another important goal that Chief Jones wanted to attain through his choice to enter the burning structure, which is to increase the firefighters' belief in his leadership.

There were relevant situational events to this story that were factors in his sense-making. For example, implicit in this event was the fact that this situation occurred fairly early in Chief Jones' leadership tenure. Thus, Chief Jones may have had a heightened desire to build their confidence in his leadership. In addition, it is very relevant to point out that Chief Jones indicated that he enjoyed fighting fire; thus, his goal of motivation and modeling must be interpreted with that in mind.

This event offers unique expressions of his leadership in that there are several goals being pursued, such as Chief Jones' desire to fight fire, motivate his followers, and build their confidence in his leadership. At a schematic level, this example shows that within one situation, Chief Jones attempted to achieve several desired outcomes with one strategic choice. In a situation in which several goals are deliberately being sought, it seems clear that the choice to act in that situation is a motivated choice. Thus, in this leadership event, which arose suddenly, Chief Jones acted out of a desire to fight fire, a desire to motivate his followers, and a desire to increase their commitment to his leadership philosophy. Despite the interrupting nature of a structure fire, Chief Jones was able to make a motivated choice that he believed would accomplish several goals.

Similar to the other events, this example demonstrated more of Chief Jones' communicative choices. Chief Jones, although a very effective speaker, is a man who seemed more comfortable communicating his attitudes and philosophies through action. It was difficult for him to recall specific conversations; rather Chief Jones spoke of how he tried to demonstrate his leadership style through action and consistency.

Choosing to enter a burning structure demonstrated qualities of transformational leadership in a very profound way.

Lessons for Today's Leader

What was incredible about this event was that it demonstrated in very clear ways, the idea of leading by example. For firefighters to see the Chief head into a burning structure alongside them, communicates a level of commitment we rarely see today. Leaders today can demonstrate their commitment by getting "into the trenches" with their employees more often. Rather than roaming the halls to make sure everyone is still hard at work, effective leaders send their people home when it's time, and stick around to turn off the proverbial lights. The other lesson for today's leader is that it is fine to make strategic choices that address several goals at once. Staying late in the office to help a subordinate finish a project can simultaneously get the work completed faster and build loyalty.

Summary & Key Takeaways

This chapter featured five critical and demonstrative instances of Chief Jones' leadership in action. The events were chosen because they captured the essence of Chief Jones' leadership style and philosophy. Overall, these events revealed that Chief Jones is a leader who is actively motivated in leadership situations by his past experiences and knowledge of what makes for effective leadership. Within each event, situational features and strategic schemas were discussed in an attempt to understand further the leadership sense-making of Fire Chief Dan Jones. The following chapter looks at Chief Jones' leadership from the perspective of the firefighters through the development of their individual role identities.

Left: Chief Jones works a fire scene in Chapel Hill, c. 2000

Right: Firefighter Jones signals a colleague during a structure fire in Florida, c. 1980

Chief Jones the newly appointed Chapel Fire Chief in Chapel Hill, North Carolina, c. 1992

Chief Jones inspects a ladder truck

Left: Chief Jones attends a live fire training exercise before retirement

Right: Chief Jones during an official event as Chapel Hill Fire Chief

Left: Official department photo of Chief Jones, 2014

Right: Chief Jones delivers remarks at a gathering

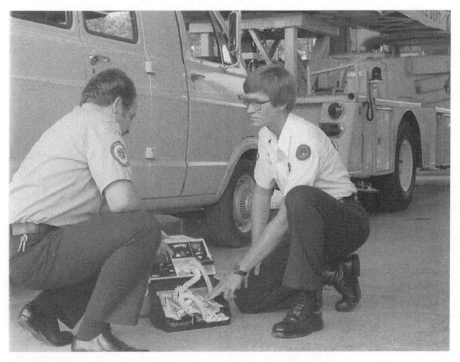

Lieutenant Jones inspects defibrillator equipment in Florida, 1980

Chief Jones as newly promoted EMS Division Chief at Pinellas Park Fire Department in Florida, 1984

Left: Firefighter Jones at a structure fire in Florida, c. 1980

Right: Jones as a rookie firefighter battling a brush fire, c. 1974

CHAPTER 4

WE ALL WEAR MANY HATS

To be an effective leader in multiple situations, one must understand the many roles each of us inhabits every day. Individuals play each role to the best of their ability and are influenced in myriad ways by organizational leaders. Different leadership styles will doubtless affect these roles in many ways. The second component of the original case study asked in what ways were the firefighters role identities influenced by a leader's enactment of transformational leadership. As indicated in the methodology chapter, the interviews with the firefighters were thematically analyzed to identify the role identities using Owen's (1984) criteria. Each transcription was initially treated as a single entity in which possible role identities were examined. To draw out role identities it was necessary to distinguish them from roles. In other words, role identities refer to idealized roles; consequently, all aspects of the job mentioned were not considered role identities. For example, one larger grouping of roles fell under the category of administrator. This role was described in terms of smaller tasks such as truck and station maintenance, and paperwork. Although administrative duties are a part of each firefighter's job, the role of "administrator" did not emerge in the analysis of prominent role identities because there was no idealization in that role. In other words, individual role identities were identified as such if a firefighter mentioned them as an idealized part of his or her job, not merely as something they do.

This chapter will identify and provide support for the existence of several distinct role identities that emerged from the interviews as a whole. Only one or two people mentioned certain role identities, while others appeared in virtually all thirteen firefighter interviews. The specific role identities were then grouped into three broader categories that captured the essence of the more specific sub-identities. Once the nature of these role identities has been explained; the comments of the firefighters will shed light on how Chief Jones influenced them.

The Organization of Role Identities

A "role identity" is essentially the idealized role that one creates, and for which one seeks validation and encouragement. However, role identities do not exist randomly or independently of one another. On any given day, we all embody and aspire to multiple role identities: parent, executive, neighbor, etc. These role identities must often be balanced simultaneously. Role identities, according to McCall and Simmons (1978), are organized in an individual's construction of self in terms of their cohesion and prominence. The organization of role identities is an essential element to McCall and Simmons' (1978) role identity model. These role identities are not separate, each unto itself, but are woven into a complex pattern of identities. That is, they mutually influence one another and are organized into a more or less systematically interrelated whole (p. 73).

Everyone has multiple role identities and each person has them organized in a particular way. The two most relevant aspects of this organizational schema are the cohesiveness and prominence of role identities. Cohesiveness refers to "the extent to which separate role identities are tightly or loosely correlated" (McCall & Simmons, 1978, p. 78). Put another way, role identities are often correlated more closely when their respective contents and purposes are similar. McCall and Simmons further argue that role identities tend to be grouped in clusters of identities requiring similar skills. Role identities involving similar skills are consequently more cohesive. The role identities that emerged in the interview analysis clearly fell into groups or clusters, which became a useful way to discuss them.

In addition to levels of cohesiveness, role identities are "loosely patterned in a somewhat plastic hierarchy" (McCall & Simmons, 1978, p. 74). Prominence is an important factor in determining the enactment of role identities within this hierarchy. Prominence refers to the place that a given role identity occupies in the hierarchy.

There are five primary factors that influence the prominence of a role identity:

1. Interaction with relevant others,

2. Commitment of self to role identity,

3. Extrinsic rewards for performance of role identity,

4. Intrinsic gratification for performance of role identity, and

5. The "perceived degree of opportunity of profitable enactment in the present circumstances" (McCall & Simmons, 1978, p. 82).

"Interaction with relevant others" refers to the extent that others either encourage or invalidate one's desired role identity. This factor is very significant for this analysis because Chief Jones clearly had the potential to encourage or discourage the performance of various role identities. The commitment of the self to a role identity refers to how much personal investment one gives to a role identity. The factor of extrinsic rewards suggests that role identities tend to be more prominent when their enactment brings some type of external reward, such as money or prestige. "Intrinsic gratifications include, to begin with, the sheer sense of efficacy in having done something with reasonable competence" (McCall & Simmons, 1978, p. 76). The final factor, the perceived opportunity structure, suggests that a role identity can become more prominent when the opportunity to receive various rewards is enhanced. Basically, we are more likely to behave in certain ways when we expect a reward – nothing new here. These factors often work simultaneously to influence the prominence or likelihood of performance of various role identities. This chapter will discuss the three general categories of role identities in terms of the influence of those five factors on their prominence.

Each role identity will be described in terms of what it means for the firefighters. After each role identity has been explained, quotations from the firefighters will serve as the primary evidence of what influences the prominence of their role identities.

Role Identity Cluster One: Responsible Community Servant

The Chapel Hill Fire Department, like other fire departments, existed to serve the community, so a natural extension of that mission to individual members was an idealized self-perception as a 'responsible community servant'. The role identity of responsible community servant comprises smaller role identities and is referred to here as a super-ordinate role identity. However, the way in which that super-ordinate role identity is specifically conceptualized and enacted by the firefighters was surprisingly diverse. Many of the firefighters indicated variation on the prominence of the self-perception of community servant, and a couple of the more recent arrivals to the station perceived no communicated role identity as community servant. For some of the firefighters, their role in the community is simply a role they fulfill that comprises many other subordinate tasks. To others, the role in the community is a valued super-ordinate role identity that comprised subordinate role identities.

Responsible community servant is a category that describes a cohesive of collection of more specific roles and role identities. For example, although fire suppressor, educator, lifesaver, and public representative/role-model are roles for all of the firefighters, not all emerged as specifically valued role identities for every firefighter. However, each of those roles and role identities was connected to the larger role identity of responsible community servant that most of the firefighters shared.

Understandably, a very substantial aspect of the firefighters' role in the community is that of fire suppressor. Not only is this aspect highlighted in their mission statement, which is posted in several locations at all four stations, it was re-iterated by several of the firefighters. FF #3 spoke about his role in the community. "I represent the department in everything that I do and all my contacts with the public and I feel we have a role definitely from the suppression standpoint to protect lives and property." FF #3 later indicated that, "the first aspect to my job is firefighting. You always come back to suppression." A different firefighter (#4) indicated that, "I think I like doing the fire aspect of it a whole lot better. I like serving my community. I like putting out fighting fires." The same firefighter also stated, "I have a role to protect people in the community, to help them from mistakes that might occur. If their house catches on fire I believe that is my part of the community. I go and help medicate the situation." Another firefighter (#5) indicated that his "primary function is suppression." He also stated, "I enjoy being in the public and I enjoy suppression." The same firefighter stated later, "I think the most important part of being a fire-fighter is the services that you give to the community...I think that we provide a service to the community and I think that we need to look at it as these people are our customers."

These responses demonstrated a mixture of perceptions of the importance o fire suppression to their role identity. For some, it appeared to be a prominent role identity because of the value embedded in it. For others, it seemed to be more of an accepted role that they fulfilled. However, the firefighters indicated they valued their general role in their community, one aspect of which is fighting fire. Consequently, the role and role identity of fire suppressor is an important aspect of the super-ordinate role identity of community servant.

Another crucial aspect to the role identity of community servant was as educator and preventer of fires. These roles and role identities are linked because community education is one of the major ways the Chapel Hill Fire Department worked to prevent fires. The following quotations demonstrate that educating the community about fire safety is a prominent role identity for many of the firefighters and just a role for others. For example, FF #10 stated, "we go out and do the home inspections, we have school drills, community education, that kind of thing." FF #12 stated,

If you work in the fire department you will routinely come in contact with people who have questions or just want to know things and you have to be willing to take the time to talk to them. You can't just say, I am not on duty, call me tomorrow while I am working. You have to be willing to take the time and answer some of the same questions, over and over again that people ask because they do not know, they do not work for the fire department.

The life-saving aspect of the super-ordinate role identity of community servant seemed very prominent as many firefighters indicated that was their main function. In addition, saving lives was a crucial element of the fire department mission statement. This aspect of the community servant category of role identities is closely linked to that of fire suppression. The purpose of fire suppression is to protect lives and property; consequently, lifesaver is a role identity that most of the firefighters identified as important. For example, FF #3 stated, "I fully realize that I represent this department pretty much in everything I do and all my contacts with the public and I feel we have a role definitely in the suppression standpoint to protect lives and property."

There were many tasks completed by the firefighters that related to their role identity category of servant. For example, firefighters indicated they regularly conduct home and business inspections. They were also involved in the schools through programs such as "Rugrats" and through the use of "Sparky" the dog to remind children about fire safety. In addition to these programs, the fire department was often seen training in full view of the public as a reminder of their presence, and it created an opportunity to answer questions. Interactions with the public were viewed as important by many of the firefighters because several viewed themselves as positive role-models for young members in the community. Although these smaller tasks do not all constitute complete role identities; they are all roles that are enacted to fulfill the larger role identity of community servant.

For a role to be distinguished from a role identity, the person enacting it must have an idealized view of the role and feel good about enacting it. This connection is one of the defining characteristics of the role identity model – people must perceive their role identities before the influences can be meaningfully analyzed. The next section addresses the second research question by considering many of the influences on their role identities that the fire-fighters indicated, among them, their perceptions of Chief Jones' influence.

Influences on the Role of Community Servant

It did not take long for me to realize that Chief Jones had a powerful effect on the Chapel Hill Fire Department. The interviewees were very consistent in articulating that he has made a positive difference at the station. The focus of this chapter is the difference that he made in the prominence of the firefighter's role identities. This section will explore how Chief Jones has influenced the role identity as community servant, and how significant his influence is when considered with the other influences on prominence discussed by McCall and Simmons (1978).

To make the term "influence" less vague, I measured influence in terms of the level of support that the firefighters felt that they received from the Chief. Perceived support for role identities is largely determined by the average past level of support (McCall & Simmons, 1978). Thus, how the firefighters were supported in previous positions and situations was a factor in their assessment of Chief Jones' influence.

When discussing if they felt supported in their role in the community, the majority of respondents indicated in the affirmative. When asked if he felt supported, FF #5 responded, "Oh very much so." When the same firefighter was asked if Chief Jones is supportive, he responded, "I can't see where he hasn't supported that role in the community." FF #3 stated that "he (Chief Jones) encourages us to be active in our community. He encourages us to be on committees, outside the department he wants representation from the department on town committees." FF #10 indicated that when it came to being involved in the community, "Chief Jones gives us 100% support." Comments like these were common in the interviews. They reflected an overall acknowledgment that Chief Jones provided support in their role in the community. For those who idealize that role, they are receiving support for a prominent role identity.

It is necessary to consider the manner in which Chief Jones supported the various aspects of the community servant role identity for many of the firefighters. It is clear that much of the motivation for being active in the community is found within the firefighters, or in McCall and Simmons' (1978) terms derives from intrinsic gratification. Many suggested that Chief Jones' support was most clear in terms of increasing the amount of time he required that firefighters spend in the community. Through such activities as inspections and educational programs, the firefighters spend considerable time dealing with the community. Many of those who joined the department after Chief

Jones indicated the abundance of community interaction compared to their previous experiences. Those who were already stationed at the Chapel Hill Fire Department indicated that, although some of the programs may have existed in some form before Chief Jones' arrival, he was responsible for increasing and regulating them.

Although Chief Jones provided support for many of the firefighters, his influence was not the only factor in their commitment to the community. It was apparent that most of the firefighters had considerable personal investment in their community role, thus qualifying it as a role identity. For many, it was their main motivation, their main purpose. As earlier quotations demonstrate, many of the firefighters enjoyed being out in the community. This fact was largely a result of their personal commitment that was bolstered and regulated through Chief Jones' programs and emphasis.

The community servant role identity was important to many of the firefighters for several reasons. The support of relevant others – in this case Chief Jones – is important because his support provided more outlets for the subordinate roles and role identities of the larger role identity that already existed in the firefighters. Intrinsic gratification was also a powerful influence on the role identity of community servant. Overall, the super-ordinate role identity of community servant is one that was influenced by Chief Jones' leadership, and the commitment of individual firefighters to the other role identities together made them community servants. It is through the enactment of the smaller roles – some idealized – that the firefighters realize and enact their larger role identity of community servant.

Lessons for Today's Leader

For leaders today, it's imperative to discover what truly drives your employees. What are they passionate about? What do they love to do? When do they feel most satisfied? It is by knowing the answers to these questions that leaders will be in a position to have the greatest impact. Encouraging and supporting employees in the pursuit of their own passion will have a profound effect in their satisfaction, engagement and performance.

Role Identity Cluster Two: Growing Employee

During the interviews, many firefighters, FEOs, and Captains indicated their desire to better themselves on the job. As references were frequently made to this effect, it became clear that a prominent role identity for the firefighters was that of a "growing employee." This super-ordinate role identity of growing employee consisted of two more specific role identities. Two of these subordinate role identities were 'advancing careerist' and 'well-trained expert'.

Many of the firefighters indicated that it was important to be promoted or in some way improve their performance on the job. When asked about what was different working under Chief Jones, FF #1 responded, "the biggest thing that I feel different about here as before is that I think the sky is going to be the limit. I think advancement opportunities are going to outweigh what I had." FF #1 later said "when you get to the point where you are stagnant, I am not doing anything good. I am not doing the department any good, and if I am not doing those two any good, I am sure I am not doing the community any good." For FF #1, the desire to grow existed strongly, and was consequently be viewed as one of his role identities.

Being a 'well-trained expert' was another subordinate role identity that was mentioned by several of the firefighters. FF #4 indicated that the "most important part is staying up on current training and staying trained because that is what saves you from getting hurt or killed." FF #6 stated responded that one of the most important parts of being a firefighter was "having the skills and being able to use them."

Influences on the Role of a Growing Employee

Firefighters felt they received greater support in the C.H.F.D. than they had in their previous experiences. FF #5 described his experience in another fire department.

> *I felt held back, prohibited, not used. I felt like I was kind of discarded and put to the side and that my full talent and capabilities did not have an opportunity to come out. Here I feel that my opportunities have come out, you know, I am not burned out anymore. It is kind of like a rejuvenation. It is kind of like getting new batteries put in you. I feel like the talents that I have had the opportunity to be used in some way, shape or form.*

FF #5 suggested the importance he placed on being useful and being given opportunities to express his abilities. In addition, this quotation demonstrates a dramatic shift in the enactment of this role identity at the Chapel Hill Fire Department. Essentially, this firefighter is now able to enact and fulfill a previously neglected role identity. Other firefighters echoed his attitude. For example, FF #2 stated that, "One of the things that we do the most of here is a lot of intense training. I am one that really likes to train to keep my skills honed. We do a lot of training here and that is one our main jobs."

Being a well-trained expert was more than just a role for this firefighter, it was a role identity because he placed considerable value on its enactment. This quotation demonstrated that improving his individual skills was important, and that Chief Jones was a positive influence on the expression of this role identity by encouraging outside education. Similarly, FF #3 indicated that Chief Jones encouraged them to learn about other fire departments:

> He has tried to make opportunities for people to be exposed to more than just what is going on in the Chapel Hill Fire Department. He's in International Fire Service and they have a major convention. Every year that he has been here he always takes a delegate, delegation to the conference to let them see others... [and learn] how to network and be exposed to other fire services.

This Captain indicated that Chief Jones provided opportunities for growth in several ways. Not only did he regulate the training program, he also encouraged his firefighters to take outside classes, attend conferences, and join local committees in order to broaden their perspective.

Another extension of the super-ordinate role identity of growing employee was the ability of firefighters to push themselves intellectually, in part by being able to express new ideas to Chief Jones. This intellectual growth fits within the subordinate role identity of advancing careerist. For example, FF #4 indicated that,

He takes a real active role in listening to what we have to say. It is not like we go through what we a call a chain of command and it may get misinterpreted or not even mentioned at all. But he comes out and talks with us and talks with us face to face, one on one, and listens to what we have to say... he comes straight to the horse and gets it straight from the horse's mouth.

When asked how this behavior affected him, the same firefighter responded,

Knowing that he takes the time to come out here and listen to me, makes me feel like even if I suggest something and it doesn't happen, at least I had a chance to voice it and he did come down to listen to it. I say well, he might not acknowledge this one this time but maybe next time another idea I have he may put into place. That is what I kind of look forward to. You can always push forward. You don't always get what you want or what you ask for, but you keep on pushing.

FF #4's remarks highlight that an important part of developing on the job is having the ability to express your ideas in a supportive environment. Similarly, FF #5 indicated that being challenged was important. He stated, "to me, I feel like I have to have a challenge all the time. That is just my personal attitude toward things. I want something to challenge me continually." When asked whether he felt challenged under Chief Jones, he replied, "there is always something new to challenge me." Further, these excerpts continued to support Chief Jones as transformational, in terms of his providing individual consideration and intellectual stimulation.

Consequently, the enactment of the subordinate role identity of advancing careerist was further encouraged by Chief Jones' providing of opportunities for firefighters to explore new ideas and challenge themselves intellectually, which enhances their overall enactment of a growing employee.

Although most firefighters indicated that their desire to improve was encouraged and supported by Chief Jones, several firefighters indicated that it was difficult for some to seize these opportunities due to the financial constraints of the department. For example, FF #3 stated that "probably the area that we get the least amount of support are areas that involve expenses." FF #6 echoed this theme when he was speaking about how the enactment of his role had changed. FF #6 stated,

> I think I have taken on more responsibility. And you know like I said, for the last six months I have been an acting officer. To me that is motivation to place more responsibility on you even though I am not financially reimbursed at this time for it, but the opportunity to learn is there. I think he has confidence in me, then you feel good about that.

FF #6 expressed that the learning opportunity was important, but the financial recognition, or extrinsic reward, was somewhat lacking. Although some of the firefighters felt that lack of money in the department was a problem, they did not blame Chief Jones. Many of the firefighters who felt supported and encouraged in their role identities within the growing employee cluster did not feel that the financial inadequacies are a result of Chief Jones' leadership. FF #2 indicated that "the whole management structure is very supportive of our people improving and climbing up the ladder so to speak."

However, when asked if there were any areas of the job in which he wanted more support, FF #2 responded,

That is probably a budget type restraint, but it is sort of efficiency. It is probably more budgetary type thing as it is a personal type thing. It is sort of ironic because they're encouraged to better their selves through schools and such and yet the department is not funded or is not able to fund individuals to attend schools. What they will do, they will make a genuine effort to grant you educational funds so that if you happen to be working on a shift, they will grant you the hours to be absent to go to school, but registration, board, and transportation usually falls on the individual.

This quotation reflected the lack of extrinsic support for this role identity category. However, FF # 2 acknowledged that the lack of available funds is more a result of budget constraints and not poor personnel management. So, while Chief Jones provides encouragement and opportunities for educational growth, budget constraints acted as a hindrance to the enactment of the super-ordinate role identity of growing employee.

Although not every firefighter's responses reflected the themes discussed in the preceding section, the interviews with the firefighters clearly showed that improving and growing on the job represent the idealized notion of what a growing employee should be to many members of the C.H.F.D. Most of the firefighters' interviews supported the idea that Chief Jones provided encouragement and opportunities for the enactment of the super-ordinate role identity of growing employee.

Lessons for Today's Leader

There are several important lessons here for the leaders of today. First, it is imperative to understand the different aspects of employee motivation. Leaders must look for opportunities to visibly support those factors, while realizing they will be different for everyone. In addition, to make that strategy most effective, leaders must be willing to provide resources to "put their money where their mouth is" as the saying goes.

Role Identity Cluster Three: Team Player

Another prominent role identity that emerged in the interviews was the super-ordinate role identity of 'team player'. This section explores the ways in which the super-ordinate role identity of team player was described by the firefighters. In addition, this section considers in what ways, if any, Chief Jones encouraged that role identity. The team player role identity category comprises several similar role identities. There were several ways the firefighters placed value on the role of team player, thus making it a role identity. This cluster differs from the others, however, in that the team player category was derived from the differing ways that the firefighters defined that role identity. In other words, the previous clusters comprised subordinate role identities, whereas the team player cluster refers more to equal role identities that were merely phrased differently.

Crucial to the role identity of team player was the desire of many of the firefighters to feel a strong sense of belonging at the station. Some of the firefighters actually used the term team, whereas others spoke of fitting in and of being a part of a family. This role identity of team player was labeled as such because it was the most representative term. This sense of belonging was demonstrated by FF #4,

> *I guess it is the team concept of the fire service. A lot of jobs it is an individual type thing. Police officers are trained to act by themselves because they get in the car and they ride their shift by themselves whereas we have three to four people we ride with. Camaraderie keeps us together.*

This same firefighter further indicated the importance of teamwork with regards to training and safety. He stated that, "you are only as strong as your weakest link." FF #5 indicated the prominence of the team player role identity when he stated,

> *Our role is that we take a part within the department and we become a significant, integral part of the family. Certain people are really computer talented, other people are really field oriented, other people are really, you know, community service oriented and I feel like I can fit into specific areas of that because I like public education... It is like you fit into a piece of the puzzle here. Whereas in other places you feel you are just a piece of the puzzle still jumbled up in the box.*

This excerpt reflects not only the prominence of the team player role identity for this firefighter, but also highlights the other identities he felt were important, such as that of public educator. This quotation reflects this firefighter's past experience of feeling a lack of belonging at other stations, and the contrasting environment of the Chapel Hill Fire Department as one in which the talents of individuals are recognized. FF #5 also stated,

The biggest part here is the kind of people. I like to work with just about everybody here. And everybody when I first came here is just like you weren't an outsider, they take you in. You know this place might be for rent, let me call over here with this guy and see if he has got anything.... Do you like to hunt? Yeah, man I like to hunt. It was just like a big family. That made me feel good when I came here. I like what I feel and that is a big key. And I think most people you talk to here will tell you that.

Other firefighters also mentioned the prominence of being a team player or belonging to a family. For example, FF #8 indicated that what motivates him "is the crew that you are working with. If you let them down, you have let down the people who have counted on you the most." Indicative of this team atmosphere was the support of and reliance on other firefighters. For example, FF #9 said, "for the most part, everybody supports one another." So, for many of the firefighters, the role identity of team player was indeed prominent.

Influences on the Role of Team Player

According to McCall and Simmons (1978) there are several factors that can work alone or in concert to encourage one's role identities. In the case of the team player role identity, many of the firefighters appear to be intrinsically motivated to work well with their fellow firefighters. However, the firefighters frequently acknowledged how conducive the Chapel Hill Fire Department was to building those positive relationships – an environment they attributed largely to the leadership of Chief Jones. It appears that his influence was indirect, in the form of providing an open and friendly atmosphere in which his firefighters could more easily build a sense of camaraderie.

One example of this influence is in the process by which the department devised a mission statement, mentioned earlier. Through a group process, Chief Jones facilitated the formation of a mission statement designed to give the department a sense of purpose. After a draft mission statement was created, Chief Jones shook hands with each firefighter and asked whether he or she could commit to the mission of the department. Not only does this process demonstrate qualities of transformational leadership as discussed in Chapter Three; it also demonstrates Chief Jones' positive influence on building a team atmosphere. By including everyone in the decision-making process, the firefighters were able to feel a part of a team, or a family. Many of the firefighters responded that they felt valued that their opinions were considered when making important decisions, such as the development of a mission statement.

Another factor that may have affected their role identities as team players was the switch to 24-hour shifts. Previously, the firefighters worked on a rotating schedule of ten-hour day shifts and fourteen-hour night shifts. Despite these long hours, it would still be possible for firefighters who did not get along to have to work together. However, the move to 24-hour shifts made working together potentially either very unpleasant or very rewarding. When a firefighter realized that he or she must work, prepare meals, and sleep in close quarters with other firefighters, he or she is more likely to learn to get along. Thus, the 24-hour shift served as a team-building device. This move was initiated and implemented by Chief Jones.

Of the three different role identity categories discussed in this chapter, Chief Jones' direct support for the team player role identity was the least pronounced. The firefighters generally indicated the environment of the station, and the people with whom they worked increased their commitment to each other. It is important to point out, however, that despite the lack of explicit references to Chief Jones' effect on their team player role identity, his influence on the environment of the station clearly affected the enactment of the role identity of team player for many of the firefighters.

Lessons for Today's Leader

For today's (and tomorrow's!) leader, creating an environment that is conducive to teamwork is the only way to maximize the innate desire for most people to get along well and work together effectively. A positive environment is no guarantee that toxic elements will not exist, however, it does blunt some of the damage such toxic people can cause. On other hand, not creating a positive environment from the top down virtually guarantees a sub-optimal, toxic culture.

Summary & Key Takeaways

It was clear that the majority of the firefighters at the Chapel Hill Fire Department perceived themselves to be performing many parts of a difficult job. In addition, some of those tasks, mainly working responsibly in the community, growing on the job, and being a valued team player serve the foundation for the role identities discussed in this chapter. It is impossible to discern all of the potential influences on anyone's performance of any role identity; however, this chapter articulated many of the factors by which the Chapel Hill firefighters' most prominent role identities were influenced directly or indirectly by Chief Jones.

Chief Jones' main influence on the firefighters' role identities came in the form of providing opportunities for the successful enactment of role identities that many of the firefighters already possessed. Through increasing required contact with the public, regulating training, encouraging outside education, and promoting a team atmosphere through cooperative efforts, Chief Jones gave many of the firefighters support in enacting role identities that were already intrinsically valued by the firefighters.

However, there is an interesting note that should be made here. When determining the prominence of role identities, one factor is the amount of time dedicated to the enactment of that identity. In effect, while Chief Jones was creating opportunities, he was also potentially enhancing the development of their role identities because of the increased time commitment. For example, the increased requirement of time spent in the community also had the effect of increasing the firefighters' obligation to that valued role, which in turn increased its prominence.

In terms of the Role Identity Model, this chapter indirectly highlights some challenging points. For example, although the model offers tremendous insight into the understanding of human interaction in everyday life, the model makes analysis difficult due to the plethora of influences on role identities. The model also reveals the variation of role identity prominence across individuals. Although this chapter focused on consistent themes, it is clear that each firefighter had extremely complex and ultimately indecipherable influences on his or her prominent role identities.

Furthermore, some of the firefighters believed that many of the roles of being a firefighter are not idealized role identities; rather, they are simply parts of the job they must fulfill. This chapter demonstrated that distinction within the three super-ordinate role identities.

The following chapter will address the inherent challenges of such a project and possible future research efforts it could spawn. As with any study, there are weaknesses that need to be addressed to make this book more contextual. Only through accepting what one has not accomplished, can one appreciate what has been achieved. To that end, I will discuss limitations in terms of methodology and analysis. In addition, the final chapter will suggest directions for future research that were made evident by this study.

CHAPTER 5

THE UNDISCOVERED COUNTRY

The final chapter has several purposes as it attempts to bring closure to the original study, the follow-up conversations, as well a look to the future. The first section offers a summary of the study and provides general comments about the findings and the analysis. The second section discusses the limitations, those inherent to qualitative research, and those indigenous to this study. The purpose of this section is to place the results further into context so that the study may be most meaningful. The third section offers some directions for future research that this study logically suggests. Finally, this chapter, and this thesis, concludes with some final thoughts regarding the project and its featured leader, Chief Jones.

The purpose of this study was to consider the sense-making processes of a leader enacting transformational leadership. This study addressed some of the general communicative choices that leader made as a result of his sense-making of selected leadership events. Further, this study addressed the perceptions of his leadership by his followers through considering his influence on their role identities.

First, I showed how Chief Jones enacted transformational leadership. By drawing on five specific leadership events, I was able to analyze some of Chief Jones' sense-making processes. The study illuminated the essence of the schemas Chief Jones constructed when enacting transformational leadership. Analysis demonstrated that much of Chief Jones' leadership sense-making was goal-directed and strategic. He had a distinct vision for the Chapel Hill Fire Department and made strategic choices that helped him realize that vision.

Through interviews and observations, I reconstructed an image of the fire department that reasonably reflected the status of the department at that time. Chief Jones was very cooperative from the beginning and very patient throughout the interview and observation process. In addition, the firefighters were extremely helpful in increasing my understanding of life as a firefighter. Despite the unswerving cooperation and help of the firefighters, this study was limited. The next section addresses those limitations that were unique to this study and those typical of such interpretive research.

Limitations of the Study

This project was limited in several ways. First, it was limited in terms of the number of respondents interviewed. Although the fourteen respondents of this study represented nearly one third of the total number of employees at the Chapel Hill Fire Department, their answers would have been even more compelling if joined with the other organizational members. In other words, the generalizability of the study is limited. Generalizability, however, is not a primary concern of interpretive research. Rather, interpretive research is more concerned with creating a deeper understanding of a particular context.

The initial study was limited by the relatively brief time period during in which it was conducted. This limitation encompasses both the observations time and the overall time of the study. Although the original study was conducted over several months, it is difficult to truly enter the worlds of the subjects in a thorough way. The participants were very cooperative and made it possible for me to be accepted very quickly. However, to gain thicker description of the context, more time would have been beneficial.

Another relevant limitation to this study was the inherent difficulty and subjectivity in categorizing and analyzing schemas. As schemas are amorphous, it was necessary to apply some structure to the analysis. The use of Meyer's (1990) dichotomy of strategy and situation schemas proved useful in addressing this limitation which is not uncommon to research pertaining to schemas. Despite this limitation, however, I believe that this study added to the discussion of schemas as they pertain particularly to emergency organizational leadership.

One final limitation to this thesis involves my bias, which became evident during the study. In an interpretive study such as this one, bias is not only expected but also often welcomed. However, that bias is acceptable only in so much as it is freely discussed. From the very beginning I had a great deal of respect for Chief Dan Jones. Consequently, the tendency to positively evaluate his leadership may have affected the results in a less than ideal way.

And finally, having had the opportunity for a more robust follow-up study, or even another such follow up in several more years, would provide even more insight into the long-term effects of transformational leadership. Clearly the effects are real and lasting, Chief Jones demonstrated this effectively through his years of service, the resulting outcomes, and his entrance into the consulting profession – focused on this very topic.

When I completed the original study 25 years ago, I was impressed with what Chief Jones had to say – and what I observed – about his leadership style and communications. I had no idea the long-term impact Chief Jones would have on my study of leadership. Far too often, leadership theories and leaders come and go with no follow up to assess the effectiveness or staying power. Revisiting Chief Jones' tenure at the Chapel Hill Fire Department afforded me the opportunity to get to know the Chief in a different light, and to delve into how his personal story shaped his leadership style. The one thing that was clear from this leadership case study is that when transformational leadership is embraced and consistently applied by a leader with integrity, the results stand the test of time.

Directions for Future Research

If leadership studies were flawless, eventually there would be no need for future research. It is the limitations of studies that serve as the foundation on which future research endeavors are built. Thus, at the conclusion of any research effort, it is appropriate and beneficial for the researcher to offer suggestions for possible future research. Further, to address many of the limitations of this study, other similar research projects are required. New studies, with varying methodologies would also prove most useful in clarifying, expanding, or questioning the links between role identities and transformational leadership.

A quantitative research project based on this one would be a productive study to conduct. For example, future projects could involve many more fire chiefs, firefighters, and fire departments in an attempt to increase the generalizability of the results presented here.

Shifting the focus of the research questions is another possible way to expand the original and subsequent projects. For example, a future researcher could focus more on the negative effects of transformational leadership on the role identities of subordinates. Which role identities are being repressed, if any? Is transformational leadership too intrusive into the personal lives of the followers? Questions such as these would deal with the bias of the current study by examining transformational leadership from a more critical perspective.

Future research in this area, of course, need not and should not be limited to emergency service organizations. The relationship between transformational leadership and role identities should be explored, both quantitatively and qualitatively, in many other contexts. The original study linked two theories that, while having an implicit relationship, have never been applied simultaneously. Thus, any future study involving the same concepts would serve to strengthen the foundation laid here.

The experience of getting to know some of the men and women at the Chapel Hill Fire Department, and of writing the original study, was extremely eye-opening. I was deeply grateful then to Fire Chief Dan Jones for the access I was granted to the department – and grateful now for the chance to have follow-up conversations. The professionalism and courage of each man and woman I encountered there profoundly affected me. Despite the inherent toughness of the job, none of the firefighters was anything less than kind and helpful to me as I conducted my research. Although it is impossible for a researcher to be completely objective, the setting of the fire department made this goal even more challenging. Interviewing people who would not hesitate to crash into a burning building to save lives was a humbling experience.

There was a clear sense that what firefighters do really matters in a way that is foreign to most people. In such an under-appreciated and misunderstood profession, it is beneficial for researchers, and others, to learn more about what firefighters do on a daily basis. For that alone, the original study was worthwhile. Conducting research in a fire department was an excellent choice that offered many benefits, both academic and personal. The original thesis and the follow-up study provide a deeper understanding and explanation of life and leadership in a fire department, and beyond. As Chief Jones stated in the Foreword of this book: "LEAD ON."

ABOUT THE AUTHOR

Peter Ashley grew up in Chapel Hill, North Carolina and earned both his bachelor's and master's degrees in communications from UNC-CH. He has worked in marketing and communications leadership roles across industries, including financial services, consulting, manufacturing, not-for-profit and higher education institutions. While in graduate school, Peter had the pleasure of getting to know Chief Dan Jones, who graciously agreed to be the focus of a study of transformational leadership. After 25 years, Chief Jones was gracious yet again in allowing him to conduct follow-up interviews. Peter has been interested in the topics of leadership and communication for his entire career, and is grateful that *"Heat Resistant"* came together. Peter now lives in Indiana, with his wife and two sons.

REFERENCES

Anderson, J. A. (1987). Communication research: Issues and methods. NY: McGraw-Hill.

Ashforth, B. E., & Mael, F. (1989). Social identity theory and the organization. Academy of Management Review, 14, 20-39.

Barge, K. J. (1994). Leadership: Communication skills for organizations and groups. St. Martin's Press: New York.

Bass, B. M. (1985). Leadership and performance beyond expectations. New York: Free Press.

Bass, B. M. (1990a). Bass and Stogdill handbook of leadership (3rd ed.). New York: Free Press.

Bass, B. M. (1990b). From transactional to transformational leadership: Learning to share the vision. Organizational Dynamics, 18(3), 19-31.

Bass, B. M., & Avolio, B. J. (1993). Transformational leadership: A response to critiques. In M. Chemers & R. Ayman (Eds.), Leadership theory and research (pp. 49- 80). San Diego, CA: Academic Press Inc.

Bass, B. M., & Avolio, B. J. (1994). Improving organizational effectiveness through transformational leadership. Thousand Oaks, CA: Sage Publications.

Bennis, W. (1959). Leadership theory and administrative behavior: The problem with authority. Administrative Science Quarterly, 4, 259-301.

Bennis, W., & Nanus, B. (1985). Leaders: The strategies for taking charge. New York: Harper & Row Publishers.

Blumer, H. (1969). Symbolic interactionism: Perspective and method. Englewood Cliffs, NJ: Prentice-Hall.

Bryan, J. L., & Picard, R. C. (Eds.). (1979). Managing fire services. Washington, DC: International City Management Association.

Burns, B. R. (1978). Leadership. New York: Harper and Row.

Burrell, G., & Morgan, G. (1979). Sociological paradigms and organizational analysis. London: Heinemann.

Cheney, G. & Tompkins, P. K. (1987). Coming to terms with organizational identification and commitment. Central States Speech Journal, 38, 1-15.

Colan, Lee J. (2009). Engaging the hearts and minds of all your employees. New York. McGraw-Hill.

Conger, J. A., & Kaninga, R. N. (1988). Charismatic leadership: The elusive factor in organizational effectiveness. San Francisco: Jossey-Bass Publishers.

Dexter, L. (1970). Elite and specialized interviewing. Evanston, IL: Northwestern Univ. Press.

Downton, J. V. (1973). Rebel leadership: Commitment and charisma in the revolutionary process. New York: Free Press.

Drabek, T. E. (1990). Emergency management: Strategies for maintaining organizational integrity. New York: Springer-Verlag.

Eisenberg, E. M., & Goodall, H. L. (1993). Organizational communication: Balancing creativity and constraint. New York: St Martin's Press.

Fiedler, F. E. (1967). A theory of leadership effectiveness. New York: McGraw-Hill.

Gummesson, E. (1991). Qualitative methods in management research. Newbury Park: Sage.

Geertz, C. (1973). The interpretation of cultures. New York: Basic Books.

Goffman, E. (1959). The presentation of self in everyday life. New York: Doubleday.

Hackman, M. Z., & Johnson, C. E. (1991). Leadership: A communication perspective. Illinois: Waveland Press, Inc.

Henry, C., & Shurtleff, M. D. (1987). Managing people. MA: International Society of Fire Service Instructors.

Hersey, P., & Blanchard, K. H. (1977). Management of organizational behavior. (3rd ed.). Englewood Cliffs, NJ: Prentice-Hall.

Hickey, H. E. (1979). Management options in fire protection. In J. L. Bryan & R. C. Picard (Eds.), Managing fire services (pp. 40-67). Washington, DC: International City Management Association.

Holladay, S. J., & Coombs, T. (1994). Speaking of visions and visions being spoken: An exploration of the effects of content and delivery on perceptions of leader charisma. Management Communication Quarterly, 8(2), 165-189.

House, R. J. (1971). A path-goal theory of leader effectiveness. Administrative Science Quarterly, 16, 321-338.

Hunt, J. G. (1991). Leadership: A new synthesis. Newbury Park: Sage Publications.

Jones, D. (1987). The role of the company officer. In K. C. Henry & M. D. Shurtleff (Eds.), Managing People. (pp. 27-39). MA: International Society of Fire Service Instructors.

Jones, D. (1994, 2020). Personal interviews.

Kerr, S., & Jermier, J. M. (1978). Substitutes for leadership: Their meanings and measurement. Organizational Behavior and Human Performance, 22, 375-403.

Kotter, J. P. (1990). A force for change: How leadership differs from management. New York: Free Press.

Kouzes, J. M., & Posner, B. Z. (2002). The leadership challenge. San Francisco: Jossey-Bass Publishers.

Kouzes, J. M., & Posner, B. Z. (1987). The leadership challenge: How to get extraordinary things done in organizations. San Francisco: Jossey-Bass Publishers.

McCall G. J., & Simmons, J. L. (1978). Identities and interaction: An examination of human associations in everyday life. New York: Free Press.

McKinney, M. S. (1991). A critical analysis of the organizational culture perspective. Master's thesis, University of North Carolina, Chapel Hill, NC.

Meyer, J. R. (1990). Cognitive processes underlying the retrieval of compliance-gaining strategies: An implicit rules model. In J. P. Dillard (Ed.), Seeking compliance: The production of interpersonal influence messages (pp. 57-76). Scottsdale, Arizona: Gorsuch Scarisbrick Publishers.

Owen, W. F. (1984). Interpretive themes in relational communication. Quarterly Journal of Speech, 70, 274-287.

Pacanowsky, M. E., & O'Donnell-Trujillo, N. (1983). Organizational communication as cultural performance. Communication Monographs, 50, 126-147.

Pfeffer, J. (1981). Management as symbolic action: The creation and maintenance of organizational paradigms. Research in Organizational Behavior, 3, 1-52.

Putnam, L. L. (1983). The interpretive perspective: An alternative to functionalism. In L. L. Putnam & M. E. Pacanowsky (Eds.), Communication and organizations: An interpretive approach (pp. 31-53). Beverly Hills: Sage.

Rost, J. C. (1991). Leadership for the twenty-first century. Westport, CT: Praeger.

Smircich, L. (1983). Concepts of culture and organizational analysis. Administrative Science Quarterly, 28, 339-358.

Query, J. L., & Kreps, G. L. (1993). Using the critical incident method to evaluate and enhance organizational effectiveness. In M. H. Brown & J. L. Kreps (Eds.),

Smircich, L. & Morgan, G. (1982). Leadership: The management of meaning. Journal of Applied Behavioral Science, 18(3), 257-273.

Smith, P. B., & Peterson, M. F. (1988). Leadership, organizations, and culture: An event management model. London: Sage.

Tajfel, H. & Turner, J. C. (1985). The social identity theory of intergroup behavior. In S. Worchel & W. G. Austin (Eds.), Psychology and intergroup relations (2nd ed., pp. 7-24). Chicago: Nelson-Hall.

Tichy, N. M., & Devanna, M. A. (1986). The transformational leader. New York: Wiley.

Trice, H. M., & Beyer, J. M. (1984). Studying organizational cultures through rites and ceremonials. Academy of Management Review, 9, 653-669.

Trujillo, N. (1992). Interpreting the work and talk of baseball: Perspectives on ballpark culture. Western Journal of Communication, 56, 350-371.

Ulrich, R. L. (1979). The fire department: Management approaches. In J. L. Bryan & R. C. Picard (Eds.), Managing fire services (pp. 68-91). Washington, DC: International City Management Association.

Van Maanen, J. (1991). The smile factory: Work at Disneyland. In Frost, P. J., Moore, L. F., Louis, M. R., Lundberg, C. C., & Martin, J. (Eds.), Reframing organization culture. Newbury Park, CA: Sage. (pp.58-76).

Yukl, G. A. (1989). Leadership in organizations. Englewood Cliffs, NJ: Prentice Hall

Yukl, G. A. (1994). Leadership in Organizations. Englewood Cliffs, NJ: Prentice Hall.

Zorn, T. E. (1991). Construct system development, transformational leadership and leadership messages. Southern Communication Journal, 56(3), 178-193.